D0193108

STAND WELL CLEAR

STAND WELL CLEAR

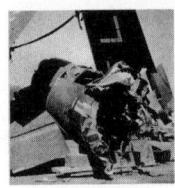  

More Adventures in Military Aviation

D. K. Tooker

Naval Institute Press
Annapolis, Maryland

Naval Institute Press
291 Wood Road
Annapolis, MD 21402

Library of Congress Cataloging-in-Publication Data
Tooker, D. K., 1926–
  Stand well clear : more adventures in military avia-
tion / D. K. Tooker.
    p.   cm.
  ISBN 1-59114-871-5 (alk. paper)
  1. Tooker, D. K., 1926– 2. Air pilots, Military—
United States—Biography. 3. United States. Marine
Corps—Officers—Biography. I. Title.
  VE25.T66 A3 2003
  629.13'092'2—dc21

                                        2002153475

Printed in the United States of America on acid-free
paper ♾
10 09 08 07 06 05 04 03   9 8 7 6 5 4 3 2
First printing

Unless noted otherwise, all photographs are from the
author's personal collection.

To my hardworking assistant, who also happens to be my best friend and wife of thirty years

CONTENTS

PREFACE

All of the stories told here are true. Some have been published before, but most are first-timers in print. In the majority of them, I was directly involved, with a hand firmly on the throttle, so to speak. I personally interviewed the participants in the others, except for the one short Army Air Corps tale from World War II in England. For that one, several U.S. Air Force friends (yes, marines do have friends in the air force) have assured me that this "raid" really did take place.

One early chapter confirms what some may recall from the movie, *Mr. Roberts:* Laundry officers receive precious little recognition but, once provoked, have been known to spring into action. The setting is the Chosin Reservoir withdrawal during the winter of 1950.

Three other chapters also deal directly with the Korean

War. With graphic support from actual photographs, they describe the dangers involved in night landings on unlit, forward area airfields. There is a dramatic story about the only major propeller-versus-propeller dogfight (YAK-9s against F4U Corsairs), told with help from the two surviving (and victorious) Marine pilots. Another story is about the only large (three-hundred-plus aircraft) air raid during that war, launched against a suitable target in Northern Korea, just south of the Yalu River. And, thanks to the fuel cell's self-sealing feature in my F4U, I survived to tell yet another story that forever dispels the myth that I was bulletproof.

Flying under false colors, bridges, and/or ill-conceived flight plans can make for some entertaining moments. I will introduce you, for example, to a U.S. Navy flight surgeon who was sure that he was at least as sane as the rest of us. His poetic way of reminding us about autumn at home, with a bowl of maple leaves borne smoldering into an officers' club in Japan, cast some doubt on that. And who but a lunatic would volunteer to hand operate a malfunctioning windshield wiper in the driving rain, while lying prone and desperately clutching the slippery roof of the rapidly moving 1953 Chevy?

Other, different types of bravery are revealed here—even mine. "The Midnight Pound Cake Helicopter Rescue" still amazes me, as it has for the past forty-some years. I was the rescue pilot, and it was one of those inky black nights over some North Carolina swamps.

Midair collisions seldom have happy outcomes. My good friend, Col. Marv Garrison, figures in an incident over the

Arizona desert that left him with half an aircraft and a lot of respect for Lady Luck.

Generally, then, the book relates to all types of adventure and is about airplanes, from 1939 light planes to the supersonic F/A-18 Hornet flying in Afghanistan. It is also about the pilots who fly them and the troubles they sometimes get into, not to mention their diversions and R&R—military and otherwise.

I can only add that this book is required reading for all pilots . . . and for that matter, nonpilots, too. I hope that you, the reader, will enjoy these stories from either standpoint.

Turning the page here would be a good thing.

STAND WELL CLEAR

1 No Tuesday for a Green Marine

It was only three weeks after my cap-and-gown graduation ceremony when the telegram arrived. I'd fooled them all at the University of California, Santa Barbara, to the point of receiving a B.A. in psychology. That's why I was celebrating, albeit conservatively, in nearby Lake Tahoe, mostly at the nickel slot machines. My mother in Claremont, near Los Angeles, had left a message at the "inexpensive" motel where I was staying: "Call home, important."

It appeared that I had a telegram from the War Department.

"Well, read it, Mom," I'd said. From the comfort of a casino phone booth I heard, in her voice: "Your Reserve Unit (Marine Fighter Squadron 123) recalled to active duty. Report no later than 1 August to Marine Corps Air Station El Toro, Santa Ana, California, for duty involving flight operations and training."

"I guess you'd better do that," my mother said, not very happily.

"Yes, Mom, I think I'll drop by," I remember saying. No need to upset your mother with the details, I figured. She was already familiar enough with the "police action" going on in Korea.

With the reporting date almost three weeks away, I had plenty of time to finish off the nickel-taking machines and, if I struck it rich, hit the quarter slots for bigger game. But Lady Luck and I parted company as the one-armed bandits had their way with me. The next few days were spent taking in free lounge shows and hitting the likewise free buffets available in some of the better-class hotels. Attempts to befriend comely female shills ended in defeat as soon as they learned that I carried no gambling funds on my person, despite my dashing good looks.

The previous two years on the Santa Barbara campus had been great, even on a G.I. Bill. We ex-servicemen were poor but never hungry. We quickly learned where the bargains were, like Mom's Italian Restaurant on Castillo Street, which offered all the spaghetti you could eat and a liter of draft beer—all for ninety-five cents. Mom loved her college boys, particularly the veterans. I'm sure I am not the only one who can gratefully remember "Mom" topping off our beers for free.

From 1948 through June of 1950, while completing my junior and senior years of college, I flew F4U Corsairs as a weekend warrior at the Marine Corps Reserve Base at NAS Los Alamitos, located in the city of Long Beach. The pay was pretty insignificant, but the flying, one weekend a month, was terrific. We enjoyed the thrills of putting the famed World War II fighter through its paces. Some of us had seen combat in the recent great war and had interesting stories to tell.

As a newly commissioned (April 1947) second lieutenant, I didn't yet have especially thrilling stories. Not many of the guys were interested in psychology, the field in which I had maintained a good, solid level of mediocrity at UC Santa Barbara. They also showed very little interest in my side job at college. My business cards had read "Landscape Engineer," but basically I mowed lawns and pulled weeds. So I listened up smartly when my squadron mates described their ships being attacked by Japanese kamikazes. We had several aces in VMF-123, and *their* stories were always spellbinding. But my day would come. I was sure of it. Now it looked as though it was coming pretty soon.

As promised to my sainted mother, I reported in at MCAS El Toro in the proper uniform of the day. I *was* wearing a nonregulation belt buckle, but it could not be seen underneath the summer service "A" gabardine battle jacket. Well, to be perfectly truthful, my shoes also varied slightly from Marine Corps requirement, but Reserves usually were pretty casual about their dress in those days. That would all change when I integrated into the regular Marine Corps some two years later.

We Reserves had no doubt as to where we would soon be headed. The Korean War was changing rapidly from a police action into a conflict that could get you killed. I guess that's what the technical difference is between the two. If you're going to get killed, it would look better in the official records that it was during a *war* and not some type of policing duty.

I was more than eager to go overseas and into combat. I'd

missed getting into action in World War II because the navy's flight training program was constantly expanded and stretched out from September 1943 until April 1947. Totally unencumbered, I felt sorry for fellow pilots recalled to active duty who had businesses to run or educations to complete. They, too, wanted to do their part, but it could mean starting from scratch when, if ever, they returned to civilian life.

In World War II my father had been a U.S. Navy chief petty officer aboard an APA (Amphibious Personnel Attack) and had made landings at Saipan, Tinian, and Iwo Jima. My mother, whom you met on page one, had saved rubber bands, grease, sugar, and meat stamps. She had even turned in any gas rationing coupons she hadn't used—while I was only learning to fly. I remember feeling, at the time, that I sure wasn't doing much for the war effort. And then, just to top it off, I accepted a commission in the Marine Corps, much to my father's chagrin. He was from a naval background; his father was one of nine sons who were either U.S. Navy or members of the maritime service.

So, as of 1 August 1950, I felt that I had a lot to prove.

The refresher flight training at El Toro was not really necessary, as we Reserves were current in type, the F4U. But they sent us anyway to NAAF (Naval Auxiliary Air Facility), El Centro, California, where we brushed up on strafing, dive-bombing and rocket firing. The temperature there in August averages around 110 to 115 degrees, so we had to fly hops beginning at 4:00 A.M. until around 10:30 A.M., when the aircraft metal became too hot to touch. It was murder, sitting in cockpits with no air-conditioning and feeling the exhaust from the R2800 Pratt & Whitney engines. But I

The USS *General Walker*, the ship in which the Green Marine arrived at Yokohama, Japan, in October 1950. This round-bottomed ship was an APA (Amphibious Personnel Attack) troop transport. *U.S. Navy photo*

think the mechanics had it even worse when the planes became too hot to work on, what with hangar space being especially sparse. The climate at El Centro was hardly appropriate conditioning, as we were soon to be headed for the coldest winter ever recorded in North Korea.

Upon completion of the desert refresher training, about twenty-five pilots and 150 enlisted personnel were assigned to a fighting unit of great fame and notoriety, one that we all could be proud of: The First Replacement Draft. With an inspirational name like that, no wonder we were filled with emotion as the USS *General Walker* pulled away from the pier in San Diego. Maybe it was the Marine Corps Band playing the Marine Corps Hymn. It's hard to remember which.

I had spent the previous evening, the final hours of my twenty-fourth birthday, lying awake, wondering what actual combat would be like. I believe that anybody headed for war for the first time has similar thoughts: "Will I be scared? Will I be able to do my job properly? What will it be like to actually kill another human being?" I was to learn, sadly.

Life aboard the round-bottom troop transport was routine except for some heavy seas encountered somewhere west of Hawaii. Almost everyone of the famed First Replacement Draft got seasick. I did not, but only because of a diet consisting solely of saltines and water. My normally bronzed color did change, apparently, as my pilot friends now referred to me as the "Green Marine." At least I thought that was the reason.

I will quickly dispense with the "mail buoy incident." This, of course, is an ancient navy ploy (like "a bucket of prop wash," in aviation circles). The new guys overhear the old salts discussing the forthcoming stops, usually late at night, at certain mail buoys to deposit letter-home parcels. Imagine! A ship, going in the opposite direction toward the United States, then stops at the same mail buoys, picks up said mail, and delivers it upon reaching port! I posted only three or four letters, just to be on the safe side. They weren't going to put one over on *me*.

But it's easier to stay green on the first trip out than I ever thought possible. How could anybody fall into a trap during the evening meal aboard ship at the junior officers' seating? (Second lieutenants like me always ate first, with the seniors—Marine captains, navy lieutenants and higher—eating at the second seating.)

A very attractive brunette navy nurse, an ensign (same

rank as mine), took her seat next to me one evening. We chatted amiably about this and that, for which I took no end of kidding from my fellow officers. The next evening I boldly took a seat next to her and our conversations continued.

John Coffman, another second lieutenant, suggested, tongue in cheek, "D. K., why don't you ask her out on a date?" Of course, my retort was, "OK, but where?"

After pondering this possibly unsurmountable task, we came up with a very plausible answer: I'd invite her to the evening movie, which was shown nightly in the same wardroom. I then informed my little group of doubters that I would pop the question that evening at dinner, it being Monday, for the following night, Tuesday. I didn't want to rush things. To a man, they approved the project.

The slim and very nice-looking nurse, one of only two stationed aboard the *General Walker*, appeared to be properly impressed on being asked out by a dashing—and of course no longer green—fighter pilot. She graciously accepted. Some of the ship's company naval officers thought it was pretty funny, but that was OK by me, their "mail buoy" caper not withstanding. I figured I would become a minor hero in the eyes of my fellow junior officers and Tuesday evening would be mine to cherish and remember.

That night, just before lights out at 2200 (10:00 P.M.), the loudspeaker heard throughout the ship shattered my dreams:

"Now hear this. Now hear this. Due to the ship's passing the International Dateline, there will be no Tuesday. That is all."

All! I guess! The U.S. Navy had done it to me again. I demanded a recount. They had known that there would be no

Tuesday, but had she? I was too embarrassed to ask, and no, we never did attend the wardroom movie, ever. I was learning, if ever so slowly.

EPILOGUE

This little episode involving a movie date and an International Date Line had a bittersweet addendum. While awaiting our military troop train to carry us from the Port of Yokohama to Osaka, Japan, I was approached by the same cute navy nurse. She asked me how long we would be staying over in Yokohama. I told her just a few hours. Then I asked why she wanted to know. She said:

"Oh, we have a couple of days in port and I thought I'd go see the Hakone Mountains and the view from the Fujia Hotel. I wondered if you'd like to join me."

I immediately went into a shell-shocked state of mind. First, I felt flattery, then surprise, which was probably followed by lust. Actually, I'm not sure of the proper order, and my short time in port made it immaterial. I stayed the perfect gentleman, thanked her for the invitation, and said something inane, like, "Perhaps some other time."

I never did ask her if she had known that there would be no Tuesday for a date with that green marine. For fifty years I've felt that she had not.

2 A Laundry Officer Goes to War

The *General Walker* made port at Yokohama on 13 October 1950. I missed winning the anchor pool by only two hours, losing out on about $400. The troop train arrived on time and we got on board and rode through most of the night to the air force base at Itami, Japan, located between Kobe and Osaka. We checked into the rear echelon of Marine Air Group 12 and were dropped forever from the rolls of the fighting First Replacement Draft. After about ten days of refresher flying, at temperatures some seventy to eighty degrees cooler than El Centro, we were told to be ready to depart Itami Base for Wonsan, Korea, on the morrow.

Four of us pilots had formed a minor clique while aboard ship. We all shared similar senses of humor, often necessary in time of war, and this ability to laugh at ourselves became the glue of kinship. The group, in order of rank, consisted of Capt. Joe "None" McPhail (so called because he had no

The infamous Wonsan Hotel, Korea—three stories of no heat, no running water, no electricity, and no toilet facilities.

middle name), 1st Lt. Harrison J. McGown, 1st Lt. John Coffman, and 1st Lt. D. K. Tooker. John and I had finally been promoted from second to first lieutenant the week before in Japan. We had often thought that we'd reached our terminal ranks after almost four years in grade as second lieutenants.

Once settled in at Wonsan, we were instructed to report to the group commander's tent the next morning. The colonel had a nice warm tent, because he didn't particularly like the accommodations at our billet, the infamous Wonsan Hotel, which had no heat, running water, electricity, or toilet facilities.

Outside the colonel's tent the four of us waited—excitedly, I'd be the first to admit—for audience with Col. Booker T.

Joe "None" McPhail and roommate enjoy the deluxe accommodations at the Wonsan Hotel. Note the stove and windows with no glass.

Batterton, the MAG-12 CO. The adjutant advised us to step in singly, by seniority. Joe "None" smiled thinly at us and entered the open tent flap. In less than five minutes he emerged, this time with a smile of genuine sincerity.

"What'd you get, Joe?" John asked.

"Two-fourteen, the Blacksheep Squadron," Joe replied. "Couldn't be happier."

Harrison J. was next and he, too, used only the allotted five minutes.

"VMF-513," he announced before being asked. "That's the night fighter outfit."

Things were going great, and when John came out, he said, "I got the night fighter squadron, too, with Harrison J." They both had been hoping for night fighters. It was the most dangerous flying of all, but when working with flare-dropping transport aircraft at night, there were always plenty of targets, usually right out in the open.

While my three good buddies congratulated themselves, I stepped through the tent flap into the temple of doom. When I emerged almost fifteen minutes later, my friends were still there, thoughtfully awaiting news of my squadron assignment.

"What'd you get, D. K.?" one of them asked.

"Group Laundry Officer," I replied, with all the enthusiasm of a death row inmate.

"You're kidding, aren't you?" Joe "None" asked. "Hell, there isn't any laundry facility or equipment on the base, unless you count your helmet." Unfortunately, he was right, as a man's helmet was his only means of attaining any bodily cleanliness or even clean Skivvies. Our utilities and flight suits were worn more or less in perpetuity.

At evening chow I explained what the kindly group commander had said.

"Tooker, we need a group laundry officer, and I'm afraid you're it."

"But Colonel, I spent all of World War II in flight training, and now I'll miss this war." I could have let some tears well up but thought better of it.

"You'll get to fly with the Group Headquarters Squadron, and Lieutenant—we don't always agree with our assignments, but I'm sure you'll do just fine." What do you say to a full colonel to counter those remarks? Sagely, for once, I didn't try. But I did try another tack.

There was, as Joe McPhail had observed, not one piece of laundry equipment on the airfield. The portable laundry facility was on a landing ship (tank), otherwise known as an LST, that had broken down somewhere between San Diego and Hawaii. A navy tug had towed the LST to a repair facility at Pearl Harbor, where it probably still is today. I ran this by the colonel.

"Colonel, Sir." I was now being extremely tactful and polite. "Assuming I do get the laundry situation under control, what would be the chances of joining one of the fighter squadrons then?"

"We'll take a look at things when and *if* that occurs," he'd replied, not at all harshly. But I remembered what my folks meant when they said, "We'll see"; it invariably meant "no."

While my three buddies were busy checking into their new billets, I spent the rest of the day doing some serious moping. The emotions ran the gamut from "poor miserable me" to a full-blown version of frustrated anger. It wasn't fair! I'd come six thousand miles just to be a goddamned laundry officer and one without portfolio at that. By evening chow the full mope had returned. Then, after a lovely lukewarm K-ration evening meal, I'd taken a walk around the airfield, mostly to observe the Corsairs parked neatly in rows, fully armed and awaiting their combat destinations of the morrow. The four Corsairs belonging to my headquarters squadron, the administrative unit on the base, were also parked there. Only two were armed, the other two obviously not in commission, that is, flyable. I'd already learned that eighteen pilots had to share those four aircraft, which meant I'd get a combat hop about once every other rainy Tuesday.

Feeling gloomier by the minute, I happened to glance out to the harbor. There were three fairly large naval vessels at anchor. One was an AGC (Command & Control) ship, the

The bombing of Wonsan left only rubble for children to play in and no place at all for doing laundry.

USS *McKinley*, and there were two LSTs out there, too, whose names I couldn't read. A light bulb came on, dimly, somewhere in my brain.

They say chiefs run the U.S. Navy, and if that's true, sergeants major and first sergeants certainly run the Marine Corps. I knew the sergeant major who pretty much ran the headquarters squadron and certainly all of the enlisted men. I decided to look him up.

"Top," I inquired, "you're aware there are no laundry facilities on this base here at Wonsan?" He was. "You're also aware that the town of Wonsan was recently leveled by the strategic bombers (not of Marine Corps origin) and that there aren't any drive-in laundries in town?" Again, he was aware and probably wondering where the hell I was going with all this.

"I've got an idea, but I'd like your opinion before I spring into action." His eyes betrayed no emotion at my subtle choice of words.

"What would you think of a couple of marines from each of the five squadrons gathering up their respective units' dirty laundry, marking it, then taking it out to one of the ships anchored in the harbor? The two marines per squadron would utilize the heavy-duty washers and dryers at night while the navy people sleep. They would each get a nice meal at dinner, a hot shower, clean sheets and eggs to order for breakfast." The sergeant major pondered this for all of a millisecond.

"Sounds terrific, Lieutenant. I'll go myself. Did you get the ships to agree to this?"

"Well, not exactly, but I think I can get their cooperation. At least I'm going to give it the old college try." Word choice not stellar here, maybe, but with the Top's backing, I'd be ready to spring, which I did early next morning. Down at the dock I hailed one of the navy's many available small boats.

"Coxswain, I have important business with the AGC. Take me to the *McKinley*," I ordered. Perhaps the .38-caliber pistol worn dangerously low on my hips influenced his decision. At any rate, in a few minutes I was climbing up the ship's ladder (gangway).

"Request permission to come aboard, Sir." The officer of the deck (OOD) returned my salute and then said in proper U.S. Navy form:

"State your business."

"I wish to speak with your ship's laundry officer." The OOD looked at me carefully while he thought this over, as it was highly unlikely that anyone in his entire career had climbed aboard and asked to see the ship's laundry officer.

"We'll try to locate him. Shouldn't take too long. Chief, see if you can stir up Ensign Pulver. (That wasn't his real name, but it paints an accurate picture of what followed.) The young man who appeared on the quarterdeck looked to be about seventeen, perhaps eighteen years old. He had not yet begun to consider shaving seriously. I knew without question that he'd be playing Jack Lemmon's role in *Mister Roberts* in a few short years.

"Can I help you?" he'd asked. I could sense he was completely baffled by being called to entertain a visitor on his ship in the harbor at Wonsan, Korea.

I carefully outlined my plan of bringing two marines aboard at night with their respective units' dirty laundry, to use the ship's facilities while the navy personnel were not using them. I had guessed correctly that the navy did its laundry during the day.

"Well, I really don't know," the young ensign had responded. Then turning to the hovering and somewhat curious OOD, he said:

"Sir, would you kindly ask Chief Saunders to report to the laundry room?"

A few minutes later, Chief Petty Officer Saunders, obviously the hands-on guy in charge of the laundry department, met us in front of several giant washing machines. I explained my ingenious plan, emphasizing the severe problem ashore with having to constantly wear dirty utilities and flight suits. The chief had only one question:

"You say your marines will do all the work? You know I can't ask my men to do your laundry."

"Of course, Chief. All the marines will need is a clean place to sleep and maybe some of your good navy chow. I know they'd really appreciate your ship's hospitality."

The chief, from his hash marks, was a veteran of more than twenty years' service. He turned and addressed my pseudonymous Ensign Pulver.

"Sir, I don't see why not. Those marines are fighting a war over there at the airfield, and the living conditions are terrible. If you're in agreement, why don't we clear it with the executive officer?"

We marched up the numerous ladders (there are no stairs aboard U.S. Navy ships) to the XO's stateroom. The commander, who was in the midst of his morning shave, was quite friendly and offered me some coffee from the silvered pewter pot that was sitting on a green velvet-covered table. I accepted, even though I was not a coffee drinker.

"Looks like the Marines have landed," he said quite pleasantly, as he wiped his face with a towel. "What can we do for you today, Lieutenant?" Before I could answer, the chief, who wore a quartermaster's rating, like my dad, spoke up.

"Commander, the Marines want to borrow our laundry equipment during the evening hours when we're not using them. They'll provide all the labor; seems they're having to wash their Skivvies in their helmets. I told the ensign here that it shouldn't be any problem for us and he agreed. We've got plenty of laundry soap, too, if they run short."

The commander poured himself a cup of coffee and watched me add four or five cubes of sugar and a ton of cream to mine.

"Seems to me like the neighborly thing to do," the three-striper said. "When did you want to start this operation?"

I replied, "Right away, tomorrow at sixteen hundred hours. If that's all right with you, Sir."

"OK." He looked at the chief, totally ignoring the young ensign, and added, "The marines can bunk down in the petty officers' quarters, can't they, Chief?"

"Yes, Sir. I'm sure they'll appreciate some clean sheets, too." There was a moment of silence as I overstirred my very blond coffee. The commander was obviously knowledgeable of the military situation and troop disposition, particularly of the East Coast of Korea. He continued.

"Lieutenant Tooker, wasn't it? As you know, the *McKinley* is the local command ship afloat here in the Wonsan harbor"—I didn't know but nodded anyway—"and I talk personally with the commanders of all the other ships in the harbor almost daily." I wondered where he was going with this. "There are two other ships anchored nearby that have large enough facilities to assist your laundry program. They're the two LSTs sitting here in the harbor. I could talk to their XOs and probably use a little 'undue' influence. After all, we're in this together. We can't have the Marines fighting a war in dirty uniforms. You probably should go aboard each vessel and introduce yourself, just to be sure."

I thanked the commander profusely, the ensign, and particularly the chief, and added for the latter's benefit that my dad was also a navy chief and had worn the same rating.

That afternoon I made the quarterdecks of both LSTs. The groundwork had been laid by the commander, and their welcome mats were already out. These shipboard visits were followed by a briefing with the first sergeant of each squadron. Volunteer workers were abundant. Every marine was only too happy to spend a night on a warm navy ship enjoying a shower, two hot meals, and some clean sheets in exchange for four to five hours' work in a warm, dry place. At

The USS *McKinley*, Wonsan Harbor, 1950: the floating answer to the Marines' laundry dilemma. *U.S. Navy photo*

the Wonsan Airfield the temperatures at night were dropping into the low twenties, with much colder weather on the way.

I went along on the first visit to the *McKinley* just to ensure that the showers were hot and the food quality in the wardroom was up to my high standards. I wasn't invited to spend the night, so a check of the clean sheets wasn't possible. This part of being the group laundry officer wasn't so bad.

Lest anyone not surmise which squadron had its laundry done first, I will confess: The headquarters unit, along with Colonel Batterton's personal laundry, did receive very early attention; moreover, my own utilities now had that clean, crisp military look—another perk for D. K. Tooker, Laundry Officer.

In less than ten days every officer, staff NCO, and enlisted man had clean clothes. The system worked to perfection, probably due to my frequent inspections on each ship, usually around dinnertime. The marines were happy, the navy was always hospitable, and I even had coffee again with the executive officer aboard the *McKinley*.

On the eleventh day of my assignment I reported to the group adjutant with a request to speak to the group commander. I entered through the dreaded tent flap, and Colonel Batterton was expecting me.

"Well, Tooker, you did it. Didn't think it could be done without our own laundry equipment. Good thinking, though I'd never have thought about going to the navy for help. I suppose you're here to talk about assignments."

"Yes, Sir, I sure am."

"Did you have any particular squadron in mind?" I was holding my breath, afraid he'd have some other group job that needed attention.

"Yes, Sir; I was hoping for VMF-214 and I am current in the Corsair, Colonel."

I was transferred to the Blacksheep Squadron that morning and flew my first combat mission that afternoon, by chance on the wing of my good friend, Joe "None" McPhail. Twelve more combat missions were logged flying from Wonsan and the Yong-po Airfield to the north, in support of the Chosin Reservoir withdrawal. For one of those twelve missions I was awarded my first Distinguished Flying Cross; I completed 133 combat missions during the Korean tour of duty.

Now they know better than to mess with the Laundry Officer.

3 The Great North Dakota Pheasant Hunt

Reaching seventeen years of age may not be any particular milestone for most young men, but it was for me. I was finally old enough to sign up for the Navy's V-5 Flight Training Program. The date was 30 September 1943. An even better reason for celebration that day: After eight hours of flight aptitude tests and more physical examinations than I could remember, I had been told by a navy doctor, "Son, you've passed and you're accepted. You'll be receiving your orders in about sixty days."

Talk about exhilaration! I'd wanted to become a navy pilot since I was eleven years old, having discarded the previous lofty ambition of becoming a fire engine driver.

In exactly two months the official U.S. Navy envelope arrived. I breathlessly read the orders that would dictate which college I would be attending for the required two semesters prior to entering preflight school. Naively I had already filled out and mailed the questionnaire that asked for my choice of three colleges, "in order of preference." I remember thinking how great it was that the U.S. Navy wanted to know my preferences so early in my career. I'd chosen USC, UCLA, and Redlands University. They were so close to my home that I could get home on weekends very easily.

However, my orders read: "Proceed by train on February 1st from Los Angeles to Dickinson State Teachers College, Dickinson, North Dakota." Good old DSTC. My mother and I pulled out the family atlas, not to locate Dickinson but rather to get a general idea where North Dakota was. I was certain that it was closer to Canada than South Dakota and somewhere near Montana. So it was.

Of current Dickinson residents, I must beg tolerance: This is a story that will expose how little there was to do in the summertime in North Dakota for a young man headed toward earning his wings of gold at the end of World War II. Possibly things have changed since early 1944, although I cannot confirm this because I never went back. The reader will shortly see why.

Upon arrival at the rather small train station in Dickinson, I was informed by some reputable navy trainees that the winters were long and the summers short. They said summers lasted only a few days, and of course they were wrong. They last almost two weeks. Ask anyone who was not born in North Dakota.

The first semester from February through May had gone well. Al Adolph, my best friend, and I had passed all our courses and had pretty much learned how to wear our navy enlisted uniforms. With a few exceptions we were all apprentice seamen, the lowest rank (or *rate*, actually) in the U.S. Navy. Alfred Victor Adolph was a neat guy. Tall, over six feet five, sporting a crew cut à la Palm Springs style, and gifted with a great sense of humor, he was a very popular guy. He'd grown almost two inches since his induction into the flight program; it had taken the navy, for whatever reason, more than eight months to send his orders to him. In the interim, he'd worked unselfishly on his tan and avoiding the draft by showing his letter of acceptance from the navy. Al played the drums in the college band, told jokes whenever anyone would listen, and probably could have run for mayor of Dickinson.

Our three-story dormitory was called the "Ship." The landing, just inside the entrance heat trap, was called the "Quarterdeck." The same navy informants about Dickinson winters and summers suggested that such salty terminology was needed to get us ready for future shipboard life. For example, a junior officer of the deck, or JOOD, wearing an armband proclaiming his lofty status, manned the landing just inside the dormitory front doors. We were always required to ask "Permission to come aboard, Sir." To my knowledge, no one was ever denied his request.

Al, being a pragmatist, questioned this procedure from the security of our room, which oddly enough was called a "room" and not a "stateroom" or "cabin." Terminology was one of several hot topics we hashed over, although most of the other V-5ers didn't seem bothered by this particular oversight. Al, being an inch too tall to legally become a navy pilot, was another subject for some serious anxiety, since the limit was set at six feet, four inches. That dilemma would be solved eventually—but that's another story.

Al Adolph, pheasant hunter, crop duster, firefighter. Too tall for naval aviation, Al had a varied career as a civilian pilot.

Anyway, to solve the question of why all this nautical crap was being administered in an obviously civilian college environment, I was designated (by Al) to approach our platoon leader, one Leo Phillips, about it. And this was another incongruity: why "platoons"? If we were going to do navy stuff, how come we were assigned to platoons? That was army and Marine Corps nomenclature. Furthermore, on navy ships they had divisions or duty sections, not platoons. Al told me Leo would know, since he had come from the real navy, off a real ship.

Leo Phillips was not an apprentice seaman like us. He was a machinist's mate, second class, and had been in the USN for over four years. He was participating in the Naval Aviation Pilot (NAP) program and, upon receiving his wings, would join the fleet as an enlisted pilot, to become a part of the proud tradition already established by the NAPs over the years.

But Leo Phillips was different in another way. He'd been in the battle of Savo Island (just off Guadalcanal) in August of 1942 and had fought while serving aboard the USS *Vincennes.* The heavy cruiser had been blown out of the water by a Japanese battle group, with heavy loss of life. Leo ended up in the water and was lucky enough to be picked up by a rescuing destroyer. Wounded twice, he had recovered from his wounds and returned to the United States for further assignment. Thus, his campaign ribbons included the Purple Heart with a star. He was a quiet, sincere man, well respected by all of us so much his junior. Leo was only twenty-four, but that was almost seven years older than most of us. He wore his white sailor's hat saltily cocked over one eye, just like me.

"Leo," I asked one day in July. "Why do we have to call our dormitory a ship?" He thought this brash inquiry over for a moment.

"Indoctrination, Don." That's all he said. When I reported this gambit to Al, he seemed satisfied. The great mystery was solved.

In our first weeks at Dickinson, Al and I had done considerable research to verify that there was very little to do in North Dakota. We double-dated once (in five months). On that occasion we escorted, on foot, two of the local belles from the girls' dorm next door to our "ship" to a Saturday night dance downtown. Becky, Al's date, was only about four feet eleven and this created a slight problem. When she and Al danced, her level gaze came about even with Al's navel, had it been showing (it was not). They spent most of the evening sitting down, chatting. My date and I were much better suited, although I suspect Marge outweighed me a bit. (I was not the cad who would attempt to learn the exact weight differential.) Both came from good, solid Bohemian families, and patriotism was perhaps the only reason for them to go out with Al or me. The ratio of women to men on this campus was 40 to 1. Anyway, everybody tried hard and survived the evening, but Al and I gave up on mingling with the coeds after that. As warriors in training, we really had better things to do.

Another big event was a horseback ride that led to an even bigger event—the biggest of our Dickinson sojourn, in fact. Al and I helped saddle up my other roommate, Allen Thompson from Whittier, California, and Irwin Bernard Meshbesher, who was from Minneapolis, and the four of us sallied forth on what could have been nags retired from some Siberian coal mine. They would trot or gallop only when headed back toward the barn. But in the course of our ride, we'd spotted something interesting that, as it turned out, could have shortened our careers. It was an abandoned granite quarry, less than two miles south of town. We were sure that its partially water-filled depths would be an ideal home for pheasant—specifically, the well-known and often-hunted North Dakota pheasant.

"Is there a hunting season for pheasants?" Meshbesher had asked.

"Probably not here," Al had responded. Al knew everything. Thus, our mission, if we chose to accept it, was clear. We would go after the big game. Roast pheasant for dinner sounded great, and with our .22 rifles that Al and I had brought from our homes, we presented a formidable brace of steely-eyed hunters. As Al had mentioned at the end of the horseback ride, "Anyone can bag a bird with a shotgun. It takes a real keen eye to hit 'em with a .22." How right he was.

We picked the hottest day of the year, it turned out, to go after our game. We'd checked out our .22s from the JOOD after requesting dutifully, "Permission to leave the Ship." We set out on foot, just the two of us, as Allen and Mesh had neither rifles nor the inclination to go pheasant hunting. I brought up the subject of ammunition.

"Al, I've only got a half a box of .22 shells and they're .22 shorts. We really need .22 longs, or long-rifles."

"Well, we can swing by downtown and pick up some longs if you'd like, but that's in the other direction." Al was right, and it was decided that we'd make do with what we had with us. The range and power of the long-rifle was almost double that of the short-rifle bullet. So, as the British would say, "we'd sort it out later."

Al had a single-shot, bolt-action Winchester that would fire any size .22 shell. My rifle was technically my father's, but he was fighting the war in the South Pacific on board an APA troop transport near some island called Iwo Jima. It was a gas-operated, semi-automatic Model 24 Remington. It was designed for .22 long ammunition, but could accommodate the .22 shorts if I recocked it after each round.

Thus armed, we soon reached the old quarry. After trudging the two miles—no horses this time—we both were sweating profusely. The abandoned pit was rectangular, about three-quarters of a mile long and slightly less than half a mile wide. Rocky walls extended some thirty feet above the water. Al said it had been abandoned since World War I. (I don't know how he knew that.)

The reflection of the sun overhead created a shimmering effect. It was picturesque, but the resultant haze made it difficult to see anything. Before we could get comfortable, Al spoke:

"Don, pheasants! At the far end, do you see 'em?"

"By God, yes. They look a little like ducks in the water. How do you tell the difference?"

"Hell, I don't know," Al said. "I think pheasants can swim but I'm not sure. I know ducks do. They're pretty far away . . . I count four, maybe five. Hard to tell, but yeah, my guess is they're pheasants. They're larger than ducks. Do you think the .22 shorts will carry that far?"

"Only one way to find out," I said. "Why don't you give it a go and I'll spot for you." I'd learned how from an old Wallace Beery movie.

Al placed the small shell into the chamber and brought the bolt home. The sound of his shot being fired reverberated around the quarry walls.

"You're way short. You'll need a lot more elevation." His second shot was closer but still way short. I had a plan.

"Al, with this single-shot range-finding, we'll run out of ammo before we get any hits. The birds are still not moving. I would have thought the noise would scare them off. But I think we'll have better luck if we use my semi-automatic feature and I'll walk the rounds up to the proper range."

"Sounds good to me," he responded. "I'll spot, you shoot." I methodically cranked off six rounds, increasing the elevation slightly with each shot.

"You're right on, Don." A long pause from Al while I waited for some further expert spotting guidance.

"Stop shooting, Don! The pheasants are getting out of the water, and they're running for those big boulders at the end. They're people!! Jesus, we're shooting at people!"

It got very quiet in our snipers' perch. We just looked at each other, dumbstruck, as we watched our possible pheasants and probable ducks become undeniable and pretty pissed-off humans, scrambling for cover.

Al spoke first. "Well, what do we do now? I don't think we actually hit anyone but that won't make it any easier to explain." He was right. Again. We were in big trouble with a capital T.

He voiced the terrible question: "Do you think we should turn ourselves in?"

"To whom," I replied, "the Dickinson police department? They'd put us in jail for the duration. I haven't met many other V-5 cadets recently with felony convictions." More silence.

The enemy pheasants were still wisely holed up behind the rocks at the far end of the pit. Al, squinting into the haze, dealt briskly with another notion that had come to both our minds. "I don't think it would be too prudent to go down there and apologize at this particular time, do you?"

I didn't think so, either. Al's reasoning was right on the mark, even if our marksmanship was not. I could easily imagine a confrontation that ended with us drowned in the quarry. The noise of gunfire ricocheting around the quarry would have been enough to provoke murderous ire in the locals.

But Al was thinking again. "Maybe we ought to head back to the Ship, Don. We can decide on a course of action on the way, although right now I haven't the foggiest idea of the *right* course of action." This wasn't like Al. He always seemed to be in the know—but then neither of us had much experience with actually shooting at real people

We picked up our brass, safetied the .22s, and retraced our steps to the college. Somewhere en route we'd decided to let well enough alone and simply check our weapons in with the JOOD, as required by "shipboard" regulations. Al's prudent sentiments pretty well summed it up. It was a dumb, foolish thing to do, but since apparently no one was hurt, it would serve no one's interests to volunteer to end our newly begun careers. The swimmers couldn't have known who had been shooting at them, right? And unless we'd hit somebody and had to turn ourselves in, they never would. Right?

No questions were asked when we checked in our respective .22s, and we repaired to our room to clean up for the evening meal. When asked by Allen, our other roommate, how the pheasant hunt went, we both merely shrugged and said "OK." What else could we prudently say?

The lukewarm, savory meat loaf and cold mashed potatoes gave me indigestion, no doubt aided by a strong sense of guilty conscience. My letter home after dinner was interrupted by a knock at the door.

"Tooker, Platoon Leader Phillips wants to see you in his room." The cadet duty messenger had delivered his message.

"Thanks," I said, wondering what Leo might want to see me about on a Saturday night. Must want to talk about our farewell platoon dinner scheduled for an evening some six weeks hence. I was in charge of the arrangements.

"Hi, Leo, what's up?" I greeted him cheerfully.

"Don, you been aboard ship all day?" he asked.

"Well, no, Leo. Al and I went out this afternoon for a couple of hours. Why?" He stared at me for what seemed like a long time.

"You guys go hunting today?" My mind raced ahead but my brain was stuck in neutral.

"Why, uh, yes. We did go out . . . looking for some pheasants, actually." I wondered why he was so pointed in his questions.

"You go by the old granite quarry?" It hit me like a ton of bricks, granite bricks. There was only one way he could know about our bird-hunting safari: He had to be one of the target birds.

"Oh my God, Leo. Was that you?" It was a dumb question. Of course it was. How else could he know?

"Don, I can't believe you and, who was that other guy, Adolph, could be so stupid, and blind."

He let his words sink in. I saw my career in military aviation crumble as I stood there, numb. Finally, I said, "Leo, it wasn't intentional. We had no idea you were people. You guys really looked like pheasants, and. . . ." Now I was verbally shooting myself in both feet, accurately. He just stood there and stared holes in me. I continued to babble.

"Leo, I'm so sorry." I didn't know what to say. His eyes never left mine. I could see his navy dress blues jumper hanging in the closet behind him. The many combat ribbons only made me feel worse. After all he'd been through . . . and now one of his own platoon members had tried to kill him, not once, but six times—eight, counting Al's two shots.

Finally, Leo spoke again. "I checked the weapons log earlier on the chance that one of our own people had been out shooting today. You and Adolph were the only ones with weapons checked out."

"What do you want me to say, Leo. What should I do? What can I do?"

"I haven't decided yet. I'm going to have to think this one over. Never been shot at by small caliber stuff before." A crack of light from a hitherto closed door. If he could write off this episode, then he was a better man than I'd ever have dreamed. He was only twenty-four but with seven years more than I, he was almost like a father.

"I'll let you and Adolph know, Don. Sit tight right now. By the way, you'd best not say anything about this, either of you. My companions this afternoon saw very little humor in being shot at. They think it was some of the local high school guys who don't like sailors, showing off. It might not go too well if they found out who the trigger-pullers were."

That wasn't all. Leo took a little more time to discharge his justifiable indignation, with some drama. He made us sound like gangsters, what with phrases like "shooters" and "trigger men." It was a kindness, actually, since "idiot" or "damn fool" had already been established.

"Right, Leo, I really appreciate your. . . ." He cut me off again.

"I'd send those weapons home if I were you." He need not have spoken. Both Al's .22 and mine were already packed for the Monday afternoon outgoing parcel post.

Strangely, Leo never mentioned the incident again. In September, when we had the farewell dinner at the American Legion Hall downtown, Leo came over and said goodbye. He wished me luck and said he was sure that I'd make it all the way through the V-5 program. I didn't know what to say, except that I wasn't going to remind him of the fact that I'd fired six rounds at him a few weeks earlier. He was a true gentleman all the way.

I never shot at any of my platoon leaders again, and for that I'm extremely proud. On the other hand, it was more than disheartening to learn sometime later that all pheasants have chickenlike feet, cannot swim a stroke, and don't hang around water-filled granite quarries.

Epilogue

I never saw Leo again. We went our separate ways. I don't think he completed the V-5 program, though; he probably figured it was too dangerous.

Al Adolph, on the verge of flunking out scholastically, mentioned casually to the senior medical officer that he was almost six feet six and therefore exceeded the navy's height requirements. He was sent to the Great Lakes Naval Training Center, near Chicago, where somehow he was discharged honorably to civilian life. He then took flying lessons, soloed, got his private license, and landed a job as a crop duster. Pilots were scarce then, and nobody asked how many hours he'd logged. After several very scary years of this dangerous profession, he moved into a much safer occupation, that of aerial tanker fire fighting. He was tragically killed in 1984 while dropping retardant from a B-17 tanker on a fire in Oregon. Yes, I do miss my pheasant-hunting buddy.

4   A Bad Day at Black Rock

In June of 1950 the North Koreans crossed the thirty-eighth parallel into the South Korean territory. This action offended a lot of folks, including the United States. It was the start of a "police action," as it was recorded in the various media, before it became a "conflict." To those participating in the action, it was a war, one that could get you killed.

Bad days are not uncommon in wars, and some bad days are worse than others. This story is about just one day in that war, which was fought more than half a century ago.

The morning of 25 September 1950 was to be many Marine Corps pilots' first taste of combat in Korea. They would hit the enemy with every aircraft available, flying from the airfield at Kimpo, K-14, near the capital city of Seoul. The targets were gun emplacements and enemy troops just to the north of Seoul. It was soon discovered that the enemy could shoot back. Lt. Col. Walter Lischeid, the commanding officer of VMF-214, was shot down and killed. Lt. Col. Max Volcansek, commanding officer of VMF-542, was forced to bail out when his F7F Tigercat was riddled with enemy ground fire. Lt. Col. Richard Wyczawski, who commanded VMF-212, was hit during his landing approach at Kimpo and crashed short of the runway. (He was rescued by friendly ground troops, although severely burned. He recovered after hospitalization and returned to the squadron three months later.) Thus began a day of combat, casualties, and courage, as we shall see.

Marine Fighting Squadron (VMF) 212 had recently crossed the Pacific on an aircraft carrier, the *Badoeng Strait*, CVE-116. After being off-loaded at Yokosuka, Japan, the twenty-four F4U Corsairs of World War II fame were flown to Itami Air Force Base near the Osaka/Kobe complex. A thorough maintenance checkup preceded the squadron's move to Kimpo, only few miles north of what was left of Seoul. The South Koreans, with substantial aid from the United States, had finally held their ground and were in fact counterattacking and pushing the June invaders back, hopefully to the Yalu River, the northernmost boundary between Korea and China.

The city of Seoul had pretty much been leveled by recent raids, mostly by U.S. Air Force B-29s. The ownership of Korea's largest city was in serious doubt. Even the real estate rights to the Marines' airfield was in question, as the pilots from a sister squadron had reported occasional ground fire during their takeoffs and in their final landing approaches. Several of the pilots remembered similar conditions at the Guadalcanal airfield in 1942 and early 1943.

Allied forces consisted of the Republic of Korea (ROK), U.S. Army ground forces, and the Marines, all of whom were provided air cover by Marine squadrons, the U.S. Air Force, and carrier-based navy aircraft. With the recent ground battle successes, the pleasant rumor, "We'll be home by Christmas," prevailed. How misguided this belief was, history has dramatically recorded.

VMF-212 had arrived in Korea only one day earlier, on 24 September. The twenty-four "Bentwings" had all landed safely and were followed by transport aircraft carrying their maintenance equipment and personnel. The airfield operations equipment was due in momentarily; hence there was no control tower and there were no aerology personnel, not to mention crash trucks and other fire-fighting equipment. As for hangar facilities, there were very few, only some abandoned Quonset huts. Anyone who had arrived even one or two days later than an earlier group was invariably greeted with "Boy, you guys should have been here when it was rough!" This routine was no doubt common talk among Hannibal's and Napoleon's ranks, too.

Fortunately, the weather was warm, making both the flying and tent living reasonably comfortable. No one knew, of course, that the coldest winter ever recorded in Korea was only a few short weeks away.

The Corsair fighters were parked alongside of the short (approximately 2,800 feet) runway. The runway consisted of World War II–type Marston matting, or pierced steel planking, the label depending on which branch of service you were in. The rather short runway length would play an important role. Moreover, although the crash crew and control tower equipment were "on the way," no one knew exactly when they would arrive. Small handheld fire extinguishers used by the plane captains as the pilots started their R-2800 Pratt & Whitney engines pretty much made up the Kimpo crash and fire-fighting capabilities. One other "missing piece" in the airfield's facilities: There was no runway lighting equipment.

Joint staff planners at headquarters laid on combat missions as soon as the combat units reported that they were operationally ready. No squadron CO would consider hesitating even a day if his planes and pilots were flyable. VMF-212 had flown into K-14 the previous day, 24 September, and Lt. Col. Richard Wyczawski, the commanding officer, had reported that twenty-two of his twenty-four aircraft were operational and ready to "shorten the war," in his words. Consequently, combat missions were assigned on 25 September. So much for orientation and area familiarization flights.

Capt. Albert Grasselli, a Pearl Harbor survivor and World War II veteran, was a designated division (four-plane) leader. His morning flight was a close air support mission working just north of Seoul with a Marine forward air controller (FAC) against a reported concentration of enemy troops. Each aircraft's three pylons were loaded with a 150-gallon belly tank, a 500-pound general-purpose bomb, and a droppable napalm tank. The 5-inch HVARs (high velocity aircraft rockets) had not yet arrived at the airfield. The F4U-5's armament was rounded out by four 20-mm cannons.

The flight had Captain Grasselli as the division leader, with 1st Lt. Neal Heffernan as his wingman. Leading the second section was a very experienced enlisted naval aviation pilot (NAP), TSgt. Charles Rutherford, and flying fourth was 1st Lt. Robert Wilson. All pilots were well trained and experienced in their inverted-gull-wing Corsairs. Their only previous combat mission in country had gone without a flaw, and the FAC had reported many enemy killed or wounded. Return to the airfield had been uneventful, and the pilots were looking forward to getting their personal equipment, sleeping cot, and tent assignments sorted out. At about 5:00 P.M. their free time was abruptly ended.

The squadron duty officer (SDO) passed the word as directed: "Captain Grasselli, you need to get your flight together and report to the operations tent."

"What's up?" Al had asked, with reason, as it was very near the end of the flying day.

"Downed pilot, I think," the SDO had answered. "Don't know any more than that."

As far as it went, the information was correct. A Navy pilot off the carrier, USS *Princeton*, CV-37, had been shot down some seventy miles northeast of Seoul in enemy territory along the Han River, north of the bomb line—the daily noted line demarcating enemy and friendly lines. Headquarters wanted air cover for the search-and-rescue (SAR) helicopter that would be attempting rescue. Grasselli's four fighters had already been armed for the next day's expected missions.

"Why four aircraft?" he had asked the briefing officer. "Two can do it, and besides, there's not much daylight left."

"HQ requested four aircraft. That's what the FRAG"— fragmentary orders—"said."

"OK, OK." Captain Grasselli's acknowledgment was anything but cordial.

His briefing to his flight members was along the lines of "Just stick with me, we'll be flying low and slow so we'll put full flaps down and S-turn over the chopper. We'll let him lead us to the downed pilot. If all goes well, we should get home before it's too damned dark to see. Any questions?" There were none.

Once airborne, the flight of four flew to the rendezvous point where they observed the helicopter below and switched to the rescue chopper's frequency.

Typical of wartime situations, flying the Marine HO3-S Sikorsky rescue helicopter was not a Marine pilot but a navy lieutenant, Charles C. Jones. He'd been assigned to the USS *Manchester,* a light cruiser operating off the Inchon coastal waters. Lieutenant Jones was on loan to the Marines, who needed an experienced replacement pilot. He'd reported to Capt. Victor Armstrong, the officer in charge of the detachment of six HO3-S helicopters, which for tactical support reasons was operating independently from its parent unit, the Marine Observation Squadron Six, VMO-6 . The choppers were parked directly across the airstrip of VMF-212's fighter aircraft.

Airborne en route to the downed pilot's site, Lieutenant Jones had come up on his VHF radio: "This is Chopper Dash One. I have a flight of four F4Us in sight, my twelve o'clock. Do you read, Over?"

"Roger, Dash One, this is Splitseam Leader. Read you loud and clear. Say again your position."

"Splitseam Flight, I'm just below you at your six. Make a turn and you'll spot me."

Several seconds passed as the Corsairs made a 360-degree orbit.

"Ah, Roger Dash One, got you now. We'll try to orbit over you. How fast does that thing go?"

"We can knock out about a fast seventy knots. I've got it firewalled now." Al must have been thinking something like, *Hell, we taxi faster than that, but then again, we can't hover.*

"The coordinates I've got show the downed pilot definitely north of the bomb line. About sixty-five to seventy miles from here and somewhat north of the Han River."

"Roger," from Grasselli. "We'll keep you in sight but it's getting dark and you blend in with the hills pretty much."

Grasselli could not hear the chopper pilot nodding his head in agreement and he wondered how far north "somewhat" was.

The minutes dragged on as the five aircraft proceeded northeastward on their rescue mission.

"Splitseam, once we spot the guy I'm only going to make one pass. When I come to a hover, that's when you guys need to make a lot of noise. No armor plate on this bird, you know."

"That's a Roger," from Grasselli, who would not at that moment have wanted to trade places with the helicopter pilot or his crew chief.

"This is Dash One. We're coming up on the location now if the reported coordinates are correct. The previous covering flight had to leave the downed pilot because of low fuel state. A bunch of small-arms fire was reported from the low hills just to the west." Radio discipline was all but abandoned in the tension of the moment.

"Splitseam Leader to flight. We'll be too low to drop any ordnance. We'll just use our twenties. Double-check all pylon switches on safe." Each pilot acknowledged in order, knowing that releasing a 500-pounder at such a low altitude would blow them out of the air. It had already happened twice in another squadron.

The four Corsairs circled lazily above the HO3-S in loose column, watchful to keep the helicopter in sight. Dash One spoke:

"My crew chief just spotted a dim light blinking about where this guy is supposed to be, about a mile ahead, if that."

"Roger, Dash One. We're ready with our twenties if you'll say when. We've got to climb a little and get our speed up a bit."

"OK, Splitseam, we're making our approach now. As soon as you can, how about spraying those hills to the west, my nine o'clock position."

"Roger, Dash One, we'll roll in about twenty seconds. Guns hot, Splitseam Flight."

From Dash One: "We've got a pretty good fix on him—if that is him. I hope the previous covering flight didn't piss off those guys too much."

Grasselli nodded in quiet agreement, knowing that an unarmed helicopter is no match for anything bigger than a BB gun.

"This is Dash One. We see him. He's wearing a flight suit but he's waving us off—don't know why. No enemy fire yet. They must be at their evening movie. We're going in—get the sling ready, Crewchief." There was silence for twenty or thirty seconds, but it seemed much longer.

"Oh, Christ, we're taking some heavy hits. They were waiting for us. Can't control this bird very well. Feels like the cyclic"—that's the main pitch control, like an airplane's control stick—"has been hit. The engine's cutting out. We're aborting the rescue. Hit the hills, Splitseam. Ah, Roger, I can see your HEI's"—high explosive incendiaries—"hitting but we're catching it from all sides now . . . Splitseam, we've had it. We've got to set down. I'll get as far south as possible, maybe to the river."

"Affirmative, Dash One. Understand. We'll stay with you. Splitseam Four, get some altitude and try to contact base. Tell 'em we need another chopper right away! And don't lose sight of the flight. We'll be joining up, left-hand orbit twenty-five hundred feet."

Splitseam Four acknowledged, switching radio channels as he climbed for the higher altitude needed by his line-of-sight VHF radio to reach the jeep-mounted home base radio.

The voice of Lieutenant Jones had sounded reasonably calm, considering his plight. What the pilots in Grasselli's flight were hearing was that the helicopter had been severely riddled by the enemy small-arms fire. His flight controls were manageable, but he needed both hands to keep the chopper headed in the right direction—south. The engine had faltered because the mixture and throttle control quadrant had been shot away. To keep fuel flowing and the engine running, the crew chief had to lie on his stomach while inserting his survival knife into the throttle linkage control slot.

As if this malfunction wasn't enough, there was another problem. Both fuel cells had been holed numerous times and 100-octane gasoline was pouring overboard like five or six garden hoses all flowing at once. Any pilot can tell you that the smell of raw fuel in such situations is as sickening as it is ominous.

"What state, Dash One?" Grasselli had radioed.

"We're done for. We're full of holes, very little flight control, and we're leaking fuel badly. Won't make it back, I'm afraid. Any news about another chopper?" A few seconds' silence, and then Jones continued.

"God, I feel bad about not being able to pick that guy up, but we had no choice. They were really waiting for us. I'm afraid he's had it. I think he was trying to tell us it was an ambush."

"Roger that, Dash One. I feel bad, too." Break, break: "Four, did you get through to base?"

"Affirmative, Leader. A chopper is getting airborne. Wants to know where to rendezvous."

"OK, Four, tell 'em to fly east, up the Han River. When Dash One sets down, we'll know where. Tell him to come up on this frequency. Do you still have the flight in sight?"

A double-click on the microphone told Grasselli that he did.

"This is Dash One. We've only got another few minutes of fuel left, but I've got the river in sight. If we can make it that far, I'll set it down on the river bank. Can you cover us? Over."

"Roger, Dash One. Our only problem, it's almost too dark to see very well. Just learned that Vic Armstrong in Dash Two is on the way and he says to hold on, and that he's solo. What's that mean? Over."

"Oh, yeah, that means he's thinking. His chopper can't lift four people, so he left his crewman at home."

Grasselli hadn't known of the severe lifting restrictions of the Sikorsky in its early years, but he was glad his good friend, the OIC of the helicopter detachment, Captain Armstrong, did. "This is Dash One. Complete engine failure. Will auto rotate into the river. Too dark to see the river banks."

The radios were quiet as Lieutenant Jones skillfully leveled out just above the water, flared, and settled into the Han

River. Both men exited the helicopter and inflated the pilot's one-man emergency life raft, which only gave them something to hold on to for support, as they floated in ten to twelve feet of water. Inchon's thirty-five-to-forty-foot tidal changes would soon have them standing on a muddy river bottom. Not knowing exactly when this phenomenon would occur, they paddled slowly to the nearby river bank and established a minibeachhead on dry ground.

"Splitseam Leader to flight: We'll orbit a little farther south so we won't give his position away to the locals, if there are any. We're still in enemy territory, for sure."

It was now forty minutes after official sunset, so dark that only the river's reflection provided any recognizable landmark. An hour passed slowly with little or no radio chatter.

Suddenly, in a loud clear voice: "This is helo Dash Two. I have the Corsairs in sight. Where away from you is Dash One?"

"Roger, Dash Two. We're a little south of his position. They're right where the river makes a sharp bend. I don't have you in sight, but I'll fly directly over Dash One's position and fire my twenties. You should be able to spot them below."

"Standing by, Splitseam Leader. Make your run." In a few seconds the sharp staccato of Grasselli's four 20-mm cannon sounded, informing everyone within miles of the river of their presence. On the ground Jones cupped his hands around a small flashlight and pointed it toward the sound of the thumping rotor blades as they grew louder.

"This is Dash Two, got a light in sight. Al, while I flare and hover, suggest you do something exciting like a diversionary weapons display. Maybe we can sneak in, fold our tent like Omar, and hightail it out of here."

The helicopter piloted by Captain Armstrong hovered momentarily, picked up Lieutenant Jones and his crewman successfully, and then headed southwest along the river at full throttle, to land safely on the north side of the airfield with the aid of the headlights from some carefully placed jeeps. For the pilots of the four Corsairs, the next course of action would not be that easy. Corsairs were not equipped with landing lights, and their new landing field had no runway lights. Jeep headlights would be totally inadequate.

As Grasselli led his flight home to Kimpo using, in his words, the "Seoul Homer," he ordered the other three pilots to jettison their napalm tanks while still over enemy territory. All of the flight members were keenly aware that landing with them aboard was, to say the least, distasteful. The burning jellied gasoline could destroy an aircraft in a few horrible seconds once on the ground.

Grasselli's wingmen all reported "napalm clear," but his would not release, either electrically or manually, no matter how he tried. He chalked up another item in the "bad day" saga.

The city of Seoul was still smoldering from previous bombings and shellings, so the flight proceeded toward the faint glow. From there they knew the airfield would be about eight to ten miles in the general direction of south.

"Some lights flickering at one o'clock," this from Splitseam Three. "Looks like somebody's put out some smudge pots."

Indeed, there was a neat row of about ten flare pots along one, and only one, side of the narrow runway. There were no pots to mark either the beginning or the end of the steel matting.

"OK, Flight, we'll make a low speed carrier break, left-hand pattern. Wing lights on at the break. Give yourself plenty of interval."

The flight joined up in parade formation, approached the runway and broke smartly, one by one, putting down gear and flaps on the downwind leg. Each pilot had to guess which side of the runway had the smoking flare pots.

"God, it was black," Al remembers. He braked carefully, not knowing exactly how far away the end of the runway was. On the landing rollout, he was aware that all the aircraft still had belly tanks and 500-pound bombs beneath their fuselages. This was not a comforting thought.

As he began his turn off the duty runway at the last flare pot, he felt and then heard a terrific crash. He'd run into at least a freight train, he knew. Actually, he'd been run into by his Number Two man, whose propeller had sliced its way through Al's tail and fuselage, stopping only inches behind him in the cockpit. Everything aft of the pilot's armor plate was completely gone. As he sat there, unsure of what had actually happened and unaware that the giant thirteen-foot Hamilton Standard propeller had just spared his life, the sound of 20-mm rounds whizzing just above his head brought him immediately back to reality. The Number Three man had landed with his guns hot and had, in the tenseness of the night landing, inadvertently squeezed the gun trigger on his control stick.

"That should get the attention of whatever army unit's out to the east," Al recalls saying out loud. As he was remembering to shut off all of his switches and wondering

What's left of Captain Grasselli's Corsair
after collision on landing at Kimpo, 25
September 1950. *Grasselli collection*

how to get out of what remained of his aircraft, there was
another freight train–like crash as Number Four ran into
Corsairs One and Two, which were now definitely mated
for life. The cannon-firing Number Three man had
somehow missed the crashed aircraft and had passed by
barely on the right side of the runway. He was safe but
embarrassed.

Miraculously, there was no fire. Grasselli's napalm tank
did not burn, and none of the 500-pound bombs exploded.
The only injury was a bump on Captain Grasselli's head,

incurred as he was helped down from the cockpit by the ground crew. Needless to say, all four Corsair pilots were glad to be alive, as were the two helicopter rescue pilots and the crewmen.

The final Black Day tally for the day (and night) of 25 September was as follows:

5	F4U Corsairs	Completely destroyed
1	F7F Tigercat	Completely destroyed
1	F4U Corsair	Very slightly damaged (and pilot's ego diminished)
1	HO3-S Helicopter	Shot down and destroyed
1	helicopter pilot & crewman	Rescued
1	Navy pilot lost	Presumed KIA
1	CO VMF-214	Killed
1	CO VMF-542	Wounded
1	CO VMF-212	Seriously burned

Epilogue

Capt. Al Grasselli completed his combat missions successfully and retired as a major in 1960 when he became a vice president of Rockwell International; he now lives in McLean, Virginia. First Lt. Neal Heffernan and 1st Lt. Bob Wilson completed their Korean combat tours as forward air controllers. Lt. Neal Heffernan retired in 1976 as a colonel and now lives in Havelock, North Carolina. First Lt. Bob Wilson left the service and now lives in Bonita Springs, Florida. TSgt. Charlie Radford was killed in action at the Chosin Reservoir in December 1950, while flying a Corsair. Capt. Vic Armstrong completed his missions in Korea and was instrumental in the later development of Marine helicopters. He retired as a major general in 1978 and now lives in Morehead City, North Carolina. Lt. Charles Jones retired as a commander in 1970 and lives in Norman, Oklahoma.

5 The Yak Attack

This story will describe, in sometimes brilliant prose, the only daylight propeller-versus-propeller dogfight during the Korean War.

Prop-driven U.S. aircraft had shot down North Korean aircraft at night, and one marine even shot down a MIG jet with an F4U Corsair. But the Chinese sent only one four-plane division across the Yalu southward that actually resulted in a full-blown dogfight. This action has been chronicled in many publications, but until now, no one has been able to tell exactly—well, almost exactly—how this aerial combat really happened. So as seen from both sides, the American and Chinese, here's what went down.

Let's say that, through some gifted, diligent, and tireless investigation, I was able to come up with the actual tape recording of the Yak attack pilots' conversations as they jumped two U.S. Marine Corsairs on that fateful April morning in 1951. With the help of several dedicated Monterey Language School students and an electronic phrase book, I was then able to render their comments into something like English—flavored somewhat, for authenticity.

We know, of course, the almost exact conversations of the two Marine pilots, Captain DeLong and 1st Lt. Daigh, as they are alive and well today and have been interviewed by me personally on several occasions. The same cannot be said of the YAK-9 drivers, so the reader must grant some latitude as to the exact interpretations of their words and actions. We all know they must have said something to each other during the brief but conclusive air-to-air dogfight. Thus I think my estimation of their communications, while perhaps not entirely accurate, is as representative as anyone's. Besides, no one else has my authentic tape recording.

First, here is a brief note on the YAK-9 fighter. It entered production in 1943 and over 16,000 were built by the USSR. Its top speed of 360 to 370 mph was about 60 mph slower than the tried-and-true F4U Corsair of World War II. The Yak was armed with one 20-mm cannon and two .50-caliber machine guns. The Corsair carried six .50-caliber dependable guns.

A flight of four F4U-4s had been catapulted at first light from the deck of the USS *Bataan* CVL-29. It was 21 April 1951, almost five months after the Chinese Communists had entered the "police action" and had proceeded to oust the army and Marine regiments from the Chosin Reservoir area. U.S. forces were attempting to push northward for the second time in an attempt to regain lost territories. At normal propeller-driven altitudes (to fifteen thousand feet) U.S. air superiority was unquestioned.

The four-plane division was led by Capt. Phillip DeLong, a double ace from World War II. A soft-spoken, well-liked officer, he was a career marine from Jackson, Michigan. He and his fellow pilots were members of a well-decorated Marine Squadron, VMF-312, known as the "Checkerboards." Flying on his wing was 1st Lt. Harold "Digger" Daigh. Shortly after takeoff, the flight learned that a fellow squadron member, 1st Lt. William Godbey, was bailing out of his crippled Corsair not far from Captain DeLong's position. DeLong detached his second section to cover the downed pilot while awaiting a rescue helicopter. First Lt. Shelby Forrest and his wingman, 2d Lt. Edward Leiland, departed for the covering duties as ordered.

It is important at this point to note that all four Corsairs were carrying full external loads, each with a 500-pound general purpose bomb, six 5-inch air-to-ground rockets, a 300-gallon napalm tank, and a full load of fifties, totaling more than two thousand pounds of armament and fuel.

At approximately 6:45 A.M. Captain DeLong and his wingman set course for their target area, their fighters laboring with their heavy ordnance load. They were at an altitude of only two thousand feet. Meanwhile, from the north, four Chinese YAK-9 pilots were headed south, looking for easy meat. Let's say the flight's call sign was "Soy Sauce," for the sake of authenticity. For sure, they were at five thousand feet, and their superiors back across the Yalu River were, supposedly, anxiously hoping to teach the Americans something about air-to-air tactics.

"This is Soy Sauce leader to flight. Keep eye open."

Let's say "Ding How" was the response from each of the three wingmen ("Ding How" can serve as the equivalent of our "Roger.")

Col. Phillip DeLong, USMC
(Ret.). *DeLong collection*

"Soy Sauce Leader from Number Three. I see two Corsairs below; are head north."

"Ding How, Three. We have big advantage, four to two. Charge gun and follow me."

In the American formation below, Digger in Able Two sighted the four aircraft above which were turning into them.

"Able One from Two, four bogies nine o'clock high. Look like P-51s."

"Roger, Two, got 'em in sight." DeLong had his maps unfolded across his lap and was attempting to spot a familiar landmark in the early light. He wondered what diabolical person folded aeronautical charts in the first place.

"Able Two, do you have me in sight?"

"That's affirm, Leader. Break—guess those Mustangs want to hassle a little. Don't see how we can, with this load on."

"Holy cow! I just took some rounds through the cockpit. Those guys don't appear to be friendlies." It was one of the great understatements of the war.

"Roger, Leader, they're Chinese Yaks, propeller-driven."

"OK, Two, I'm split-essing out of here. Turn into them. Can't believe they overshot us so badly." DeLong pushed everything to the firewall in a desperate effort to pick up speed. At the same time he flailed at the loose maps now floating weightless around the cockpit. What a hell of time to get hit—while map reading.

From my closely guarded and irreplaceable Chinese tape: "Soy Sauce to flight, we overshoot. Corsairs go too slow. Jane's Aircraft Almanac make mistake. Number Four, you have enemy plane behind you. Suggest do something."

Wingman Digger Daigh had not been idle, nor had he had to deal with map folding exercises. He had tried (but failed) to release his 500-pound bomb and napalm but did charge his six .50-caliber guns. In overshooting, the fourth Yak had pulled up sharply, trying to keep the Corsair leader in sight. In so doing he crossed directly in front of Daigh, who promptly sent a burst of fifties into the wing root of the Yak. The enemy aircraft immediately streamed smoke, then flames, and dove straight into the ground. Now the odds were three to two.

"Break right, Leader!" Daigh had seen another Yak perform the unbelievable overshoot maneuver, which by turning sharply allowed DeLong's gun sight to frame the Number Three Yak. A quick accurate burst smashed into the Yak and sent it spinning into the ground. It crashed and burned less than half a mile from where Daigh's victim had hit.

"Soy Sauce Two from Leader. Odds not so good. We go north. You see me, Number Two?"

"Ding How, Leader, but Corsair stay on my tail. Why they go so slow? We overshoot too much."

The air battle continued but the obviously superior airmanship of the Americans began to tell. Whenever the Yaks would make a run on either of the two Corsairs, who were protecting each other's tails, their excessive speed would allow the Marine pilots to turn inside of them. Thus, the Yaks could never pull enough lead to score any hits. Daigh pulled in behind the Number Two Yak and sprayed the enemy aircraft thoroughly. Smoke issued from beneath the engine as he hightailed it for China.

"Soy Sauce Leader. Have overheat engine. Must unfortunately speak goodbye." There's nothing on my confidential tape from the Chinese leader. I guess he realized that perhaps he'd tackled the wrong Corsair twosome. Indeed he had. Lieutenant Daigh was one of the best dogfighting pilots in the Marine squadron and had almost a thousand hours in the F4U. Even worse for Soy Sauce Leader, had he but known, Captain DeLong was a double ace in World War II, having shot down eleven enemy aircraft. The last Yak headed north at full throttle.

"Able Two, keep your eye on that smoker. I don't think he wants any more, though. I'm closing on their leader." So saying, DeLong elevated the nose of the aircraft, sending a hail of bullets over the top of the fleeing Yak, knowing he was well out of effective range.

As he watched, startled, he saw the pilot open his canopy and bail out. He landed almost immediately and appeared to be all right. DeLong radioed for a chopper to pick up the downed Chinese pilot, but the request was never acknowledged over the radio. (There is no official record of this pilot ever being captured or recovered.)

The streaking surviving YAK-9 continued north, now emitting volumes of black smoke.

"Able One, I'm marginal on fuel. Don't think I've enough left to give chase. I've been firewalled the whole time."

"Roger, Two, let's quit while we're ahead. I see you've still got all your ordnance."

"Roger, so do you. Well, in the heat of battle. . . ." Nothing more needed to be said, as they later dropped their ordnance in the ocean on the return trip to the carrier. Oddly, by not jettisoning it and flying so slowly as a result, they had inadvertently confused the Chinese pilots in the Soy Sauce flight into continually overshooting the Corsairs.

Epilogue

The wreckage of the fourth YAK-9 was later located on 26 April by United Nations Forces in some shallow water on the western coast of North Korea. A Chinese pilot, believed to be the one in question, was identified as twenty-seven-year-old Lt. Yun Hong Yo of the Second Company, 1st Battalion, Pursuit Regiment, 813 Nan King Army Corps, as reported in *The Hook* magazine, Fall 1986 issue.

This upgraded First Lieutenant Daigh's probable to a confirmed total of two. Captain DeLong's total of downed enemy aircraft was now officially thirteen. The Chinese pilot who bailed out was never found. It was the opinion of both Marine pilots that the enemy airmen had more courage than skill. They had misused their numerical superiority and altitude advantage and failed to attack from out of the sun.

Captain DeLong was awarded the Silver Star for his role in the 21 April 1951 action and retired as a colonel in 1969. He presently resides with his wife, Katherine, in Treasure Island, Florida.

Harold "Digger" Daigh received his second Distinguished Flying Cross for his actions. Upon completion of his Korean combat tour, he shared a bachelor pad in Laguna Beach, California, with me. (These adventures are the subject of another book.) Digger left the Marine Corps at 1953 after ten years of service and resumed his career in automobile racing. He now lives with his wife, Dorothy, in Rolling Hills Estates, California.

6 North Korea's Biggest Air Raid—Sinuiju

I t was my seventy-sixth combat mission, and it was nearly my last. The Korean War was almost a year old, and the bomb line (a new term for the front lines) was pretty much stabilized—although "stalemated" would be a better word— in the general vicinity of the thirty-eighth parallel.

As a member of Marine Fighter Squadron 212, I was looking forward to finally participating in something big, rather than our usual two- and four-plane formations flying close air support missions in conjunction with our ground Marine forces. Most often we flew in two-plane sections north of the bomb line looking for targets of opportunity.

Rumor had it that our squadron of twenty-four F4U-5 Corsairs would be a part of a joint effort of perhaps three hundred aircraft. For once the rumor was true. Air force and navy pilots flying from carriers and we marines were to

Capt. Bob Stigall a few months earlier, aboard the USS *Bataan*, CVL 29, February 1951.

strike a target of some sort all the way north to the Yalu River, that body of water separating North Korea from mainland China.

We breakfasted at our fighter strip, K-3 (Pohang Ni Dong), which was located about eighty miles north of Pusan, the southern tip of Korea. Our squadron was to put every available aircraft into the air and fly about 180 miles north to another airfield near Seoul with the enchanting name of K-16. Every airfield in-country had a number along with the "K" designation. The date was 9 May 1951.

We'd taken off with twenty-four fighter bombers just before dawn, and as we joined up in formation we were privileged to watch a gorgeous sunrise. My flight of four was led by Capt. Bob Stigall, a reserve officer who'd had two tours in the South Pacific in World War II. He was a very close friend with sparkling (always it seemed) blue eyes and a sense of humor unparalleled. On his wing was another captain, who preferred to fly in that position. Peter Van Ness was a regular or career marine. Soft-spoken, very short in stature, and quite handsome, he usually carried a stack of seat cushions to boost him up to "cockpit-eye level," as he put it. Peter Van Ness taught me how four queens always beat four tens in a poker game of seven-card stud (an expensive lesson).

Leading the second section in the Number Three position was the star of this story, me. I was a first lieutenant. but since I had completed seventy-five combat missions, I'd been designated as a division leader. Captain Stigall had asked earlier if I wanted to lead the four-plane flight—a nice gesture, I thought.

"No, Bob, I'd probably get us lost," I said. He'd agreed, with that unmistakable twinkle in his eyes.

On my wing as the Number Four man was a brand-new "nugget" (second lieutenant) named J. J. Prior. He looked exactly like James Dean, the movie actor. Since Dean entered the scene later in this life, it would be better to say that James Dean looked like J. J., only Prior was even more handsome. I'd asked for him to be assigned as my permanent wingman for two reasons: One, I liked him and two, I wanted to get him through the war and home in one piece. Although at twenty-four I was only four years older, we both felt that he was like my little brother.

As we flew up the center of the Korean Peninsula, I wondered how the day would end. To be a part of a huge raid (it was to be the largest in the war, with over 320 aircraft participating) was especially thrilling, and I wondered how it would compare with the five-hundred- and thousand-plane raids over Europe in World War II. I never was able to draw a logical comparison.

Our destination, K-16, was a large airfield with room to park, service, and arm many aircraft. We'd taken off from K-3 with just a belly tank and were to arm the Corsairs with bombs and rockets at K-16. After the briefing, I remember thinking how prudent this was, not exactly being fond of landing with two 500-pound bombs shackled below. Even though they would be armed "safe," accidents did happen.

A word from the sponsor here (me) is due to orient any reader who wasn't able to participate in the Chosin Reservoir withdrawal in November–December of 1950. When the Chinese communists entered the Korean conflict during this freezing-cold winter period, it became prudent to vacate the northern parts of the country, mainly because our ground forces were outnumbered by at least a hundred to one. Marine aviation units regrouped back in Japan, deploying around Christmastime to two small carriers and to two major airstrips in the southern parts of Korea, Pusan (K-1) and Pohang Ni Dong (K-3). Thus, after falling back from the *northern* part of the peninsula, our armed forces began the long trek of recapturing the lost terrain from the *southern* tip of Korea. Our missions were in support of this effort.

Seoul, the capital of Korea, is located on the west coast and roughly halfway between Pusan and the boundary Yalu River. Around what was left of the capital city there were three major airfields: Suwon (K-13) a little to the south, Seoul City (K-16), and Kimpo (K-14). This story revolves around two of the three airfields, K-16 and K-14.

Our flight of six groups of four aircraft approached our first destination in perfect formation. We particularly wanted to look professional when other squadrons were lurking around. Nothing is worse than for another pilot, usually at happy hour, to casually mention that "Your division looked a bit shabby over the break." So VMF-212 Devilcats (our nickname) worked hard to fly nice, tight wing positions. We broke smartly over the numbers in groups of four, following behind our squadron commanding officer, Lt. Col. Claude H. Welch, a career officer from the Deep South. "Windy" Welch was a popular, well-liked CO who'd gone through flight training as a major and thus had very little flying experience. I'd given him his first familiarization and area checkout flights, for which I thought I deserved a certain amount of recognition and acclaim. He always called me "Mister Tooka," and we became close friends, as only a first lieutenant reserve officer and regular USMC Lt. Col. could become.

Once on the ground, a "follow-me" jeep led us to our parking area adjacent to the largest hangar on the field. Immediately to our right were several squadrons of New Zealand and Australian P-51s. They were the crazies of the Korean conflict, and they flew like it was Air Show Sunday every day. They were great guys, good pilots and fun to be around. They flew tighter wing positions than anyone else, but we marines always felt that if the leader ever got shot down, the other wingmen would become hopelessly lost and have to bail out. You can't read a map very well with your propeller three feet from the leader's canopy. Not to be shown up by the boys from Down Under, we, at the colonel's command, did what any self-respecting naval pilot would do: We folded our wings when taxiing. This always brought a "I say, good show," or "Bang on, ole chap."

After postflighting our F4Us, we were directed to the hangar where the brass was preparing for the big briefing. As we milled around smartly awaiting the word, the armament guys were busily pushing the bomb carts under the ordnance pylons and attaching, casually I thought, 500-pound bombs to each aircraft. The third pylon with the 150-gallon belly tank had already been attached back at K-3, and it was topped off along with the main fuel cell. On the F4U-5 the main held 250 gallons of 115/145 high-octane fuel. (Most cars run on 87 to 92 octane.) This gasoline is the most volatile of all aircraft fuels, not counting those used in air races (relished by more crazies) where things like ether and nitroglycerine are blended in.

"Gentlemen, please take your seats." The MAG-12 (Marine Air Group 12) executive officer was about to speak. Lt. Col. Don Yost looked like a short Gregory Peck fresh from *Twelve O'Clock High*. His face was deeply lined, and his closely cropped gray hair gave him a perfect hard military look. He wore the typical naval aviator's leather flight jacket, had a cigarette in hand, and was in total command. His deep voice and the seriousness of the impending mission had everyone's complete attention. Colonel Yost was to lead the mission, and he proceeded to brief us as to "why we're all gathered here today"; you could have heard the proverbial pin drop. Even the P-51 pilots were paying attention.

"Gentlemen," he began, "today's mission is the first of its kind so far in this war." (He did not say "conflict.")

"Our intelligence has learned about and photographed a large concentration of disassembled aircraft, engines, wings, fuselages—all kinds of parts, under some very clever and extensive camouflage. Obviously it wasn't clever enough, as our photo interpreters were able to confirm this buildup. I can't tell you men how important it is to eliminate this threat. If the Chinese Communists are allowed to assemble these aircraft, they will be able to disrupt our entire war effort. Given enough aircraft, located just a few miles from a safe haven, they could make one hell of a dent in our present air superiority." He paused to let all of this sink in.

Colonel Yost continued:

"We are going to hit that area today hard!" He paused again for effect, took a deep drag on his cigarette and slowly exhaled, while we held our collective breath.

"We'll be a part of an operation that will be comprised of approximately 320 aircraft. The Air Force F-86s from K-13 will provide continuous high cover and we do expect the MIGs to try and spoil our show. The navy will rendezvous with us with F4Us, ADs and F9Fs at Point X-ray." (He pointed to a spot on the large map that was tacked to a portable blackboard.)

"The Marine F9Fs along with the Air Force F-80s and F-84s will go in first due to their limited fuel. The props, which I will lead, will go in last. The P-51s will precede Colonel Welch's squadron." That was VMF-212, my outfit. "The times of departure from Point X-ray will be on my command." He then listed each unit's approach sequence to the target area.

"You can copy down the exact coordinates of the target complex after the briefing. You'll note this area is only a few miles from the Yalu. You'll probably be able to see the MIGs taking off to the north across the river or at least their dust." The MIG fields had dirt runways, and we would, in fact, see them.

"I must remind all you fighter jocks that they"—the MIGs—"are the responsibility of the F-86 Sabre Jets. Your mission, your *only* mission, is to drop bombs, rockets and strafe." Some audible groans were heard from the Marine pilots. "We'll have what sun there is at our backs. Make your runs as close to a 270-degree heading as possible."

"Some final items," Colonel Yost continued. "All pullouts will be to the left. Nobody pulls out to the right. That would put you into China, and that's not in the rules." He was referring to the rules of engagement set forth by the policy makers in Washington. No one could cross the Yalu and go after enemy aircraft or their airfields.

"One other thing: I want everyone out of their run by twenty-five hundred feet. No lower. The AA [antiaircraft fire] is unknown but estimated to be moderate to intense, with some pretty heavy stuff. We don't think it's radar controlled, but intelligence predicts plenty of 37-mm, maybe heavier." He paused again and crushed the remaining part of his cigarette under his flight boot. "Gentlemen, this is a one-run, one-shot mission. Get in, get out, and come home. Major Riley will brief you on the rescue facilities, weather, and communication procedures. Good luck!"

He stepped off the slightly raised platform and walked behind us to the rear of the hangar area. The group operations officer then provided the nuts and bolts of the mission—which squadrons would bomb first, the who-follows-who sequences. The air force, as Colonel Yost had said, would lead the show, followed by the navy carrier boys. The F-51s would be next and finally the good guys—us. My unit would be the "Tail-end Charlie" squadron, and our division, with Captain Stigall leading, would bomb the target, dead last. I remember thinking, as Colonel Welch briefed our twenty-four, pilots that by the time we struck our mighty blow for freedom, the target would already be blown to smithereens. Peter Van Ness, always the pessimist, except when he held four queens, had a different viewpoint.

"By the time we get there, the AA gunners will have us boresighted. They'll have figured our dive angle and air speed." I hoped he was wrong.

Lunch was not being served to our rather impressive gathering. The P-51 pilots were laughing and joking as if this were a perfect picnic outing. Perhaps for them it was. Most of our pilots were munching on crackers and stale chocolate bars from their flight suit pockets. We all took a swig from the ever present Lister bag, the large canvas water cooler hanging conveniently nearby, and then attended to personal needs, always necessary prior to a long flight. After basic requirements were completed, we headed toward the refueled and rearmed F4Us. I noticed for the first time that the side number on my plane was thirteen. *Best not be superstitious*, I remember thinking.

As we prepared to man aircraft, my wingman, J. J. Prior, asked, "D. K., are you nervous?" It was a tough question; of course I was nervous—who wouldn't be? But I wanted to provide some sense of reassurance for him, as it was only his tenth or eleventh mission.

"Yeah, a little, J. J., but with this many Little Friends around, I'm sure we'll be fine. Just stick with me, stay in tight except in the run itself. Fire your rockets first and then concentrate on your bomb release. Remember pull out by twenty-five hundred feet and check all your switches on safe on the join-up." He nodded, with some degree of reticence, but I'd given him something else to think about. I was sure he trusted my judgment and would do his best to guard himself *and* my six o'clock.

We took off in sections (pairs) and joined up in a running rendezvous headed north to the Yalu to participate in the largest air raid conducted thus far during the Korean War. The distance to the IP, or initial point, was about 240 nautical miles. Each plane in our squadron carried two 500-pound bombs and a 150-gallon droppable belly tank. (The F4U-5s had three pylons, the F4U-4s only two.) We also carried eight 5-inch HVARS—high-velocity aircraft rockets—and full 20-mm ammo, six hundred rounds.

Fuel was not a problem, nor was the distance excessive. With a belly tank and a full main, we had enough petrol for at least five hours of flight, depending, of course, on the power settings used. We all would use full power during our bombing run and the pullout while departing the area.

Our squadron's formation looked professional, with each aircraft tucked in nicely. Even the P-51 blokes must be impressed, I thought. As we approached the target area, I reviewed everything mentally. The weather was not a factor, a few high clouds and some of the ever present haze limiting the visibility to around fifteen to twenty miles. The armament switches were carefully noted, along with which pylon had bombs or belly tank. My final thought as we neared the

IP was that the rescue helicopters' range was only about fifty to sixty nautical miles north of the bomb line. If you had to bail out beyond their radius of action, you'd best be prepared to spend some days as a guest of the Chinese Communists, whose property you'd just tried to bomb off the face of the earth.

"Splitseam Flight, this is Splitseam One [Colonel Welch]. We'll orbit left hand, at twelve thousand. Expect depart X-Ray in approximately one zero minutes. Out." Precisely ten minutes later all twenty-four bentwings wheeled majestically toward the west and took some space separation. As I looked ahead, I could clearly see the target area, now ablaze with smoke and flames. A few seconds later I rolled into the dive at about a forty-five-degree angle and set up the proper mil lead in the gun sight. I fired the eight rockets in pairs, pickled off the two bombs, and switched to guns, spraying the twenties at the general area like a madman.

As I pulled out, I ran into a freight train—at least it felt like running into something almost that substantial. I knew it wasn't slipstream or another aircraft. I turned left (south) and consulted the instruments on the panel a few inches away. They said nothing, but my wingman, whom I could see in the mirror, did speak.

"Splitseam Two Three, you're trailing smoke." OK, I thought, but what kind of smoke? Fire, fuel, hydraulic fluid—they all look alike when streaming from an airplane.

"Slow down, Two Three, so I can catch up." I throttled back immediately, realizing I still had all the levers on the throttle quadrant in their full forward position. It was then that I discovered the one instrument that I had not consulted, the fuel gauge. It had registered almost full at the beginning of the bombing run. It was now visibly moving toward the little numbers. It was painfully obvious what the earlier collision on the pullout was—antiaircraft fire had hit the main fuel cell and fuel was pouring out of the bottom of the fuselage. I punched the mike button on the throttle.

"Switch to guard channel." A moment's pause, then: "Splitseam Two One, Two Two, and Two Four. Bob, I've taken a hit in the main fuel cell for sure. Twenty-four, can you verify?"

"Affirm, Two Three. It looks like thin smoke," though J. J. apparently had never seen a fuel leak while airborne.

"OK, Two Three from Two One Leader. What's your fuel state now?"

"When I first noticed it, it was around two hundred–plus gallons. Now it's already down to just over a hundred and fifty. Needle's still moving."

"We're way too far north for any chopper help. Do you want to slow down or speed up?" Bob asked. I'd thought this over. At slow speeds the engine used less fuel, but the leak was the dominant consideration. There were two demands being made on the fuel tank simultaneously. The belly tank had been hit also, probably by the same piece of flak. J. J. had reported this, and I'd jettisoned the belly tank to reduce aerodynamic drag.

"Bob, I think I'm screwed. It's down to a hundred and thirty gallons and it's still moving. I don't believe there'll be enough to even make the coast." Bailing out somewhere along the west coast was always better from a rescue point of view. A ship could transport a rescue helo near enough to effect a rescue, maybe.

We were back up to a fast cruise speed, about 350 knots,

with a little more than 160 miles still to go. The silence was heavy as everyone tried to think of some way to help.

"Seventy gallons," I'd reported to the nonanswering flight of three. What was there to say? In another ten to fifteen minutes I'd be bailing out over enemy territory and to certain capture. The condemned man ate a hearty meal. My wingmen, like me, were powerless to do anything.

"What state, Two Three?" Captain Stigall asked. As my eyes returned to the fate-determining gas gauge, I stared unbelievingly. The gauge was just about the same as it had been a few minutes earlier. It still read almost sixty gallons.

"This is Two Three. I'm throttling back. J. J., can you still see smoke coming out?"

"Wait one, Two Three, I'll check." He slid underneath my aircraft and after a few seconds reported:

"That's a negative, Two Three. It looks like it's stopped."

"I hope so. The gauge isn't moving any more. I'm reducing to sixteen hundred rpm and twenty inches of manifold pressure." Our airspeed decreased at once to barely 150 knots. At max range and endurance maybe I could get back, at least to a place where I could bail out and possibly be rescued. I did some fast mental calculations. The Corsair burned almost seventy gallons per hour at normal cruise and maybe fifty to fifty-five at max endurance. I wished I'd done a little more flying at slow speeds to know just how economical the F4U could be (I always liked to go everywhere at full throttle).

With about 160 miles remaining, perhaps more, at 2.5 miles per minute, that would get me almost to the bomb line. It is harder to figure out miles, minutes, and fuel remaining when your life is on the line. But each time I ran the math the answer came out the same . . . about five minutes or fifteen miles short, take your choice.

In thirty minutes the gas gauge read just above the thirty-gallon tick, and my three wingmen were nestled in so close I could read the anxiety on their faces. I wondered just how casual I looked and sounded to them.

"We're only about forty-five miles or so north of the nearest airfield, K-14," Bob reported, some twenty minutes later. "I think the field is in friendly hands, but I'm not really sure. The situation there changes almost daily. Don't believe you can reach K-16. What do you think?"

"Bob, I don't have much choice. The gauge agrees with you. Stay with me and I'll try to make it to Kimpo [K-14]."

"Roger that, Two Three. I've notified air sea rescue but they're at least twenty minutes away. Suggest you try K-14, or . . . ." After a long pause, he added, "Or you can bail out here while you still have power."

I chose to follow the basic rule in airplane flying: Keep it flying as long as it can still fly. As I remembered this cardinal axiom, I spotted the plateau on which the K-14 airfield was located, dead ahead.

"Don't put your wheels down until you got the field made," the division leader admonished.

On the long final straight-in I locked the canopy open and increased the power slightly, a precaution in case of a wave-off. As I crossed over the end of the runway and gently touched the wheels down, all hell broke loose. Red balls from the right zinged across the runway in front of me. I figured the friendlies were on my right to the south, so why were they shooting at me, one of the good guys?

Then, as I was rolling down the Marston matting runway,

more red balls crossed over my head from the left side. I had landed smack dab in the middle of a fierce firefight, apparently over who should be the rightful owner of the airstrip.

Quickly I increased power, raised the wheels and, to coin a phrase, got the hell out of there. Neither side wanted to stop their nasty fighting long enough for me to land.

"I'm back up to nine hundred feet, Splitseam Leader. There was no welcome mat out down there."

"I know, Two Three. Sorry about that. Did you get hit? And what's your fuel state?"

"No, and it's reading zero, if the gauge is accurate. Call K-16 and tell 'em I'm going to try for their field. I'll stay at nine hundred feet"—the recommended minimum altitude for a Corsair bailout—"and make a straight-in. And Bob, don't give 'em that 'wing and a prayer' bit." Yes, Virginia, there *is* humor in battle—relief from otherwise deadly tension.

The map showed K-16 to be only about ten or twelve miles southeast, but it was an anxious four minutes until I spotted the runway. At three miles I was cleared by the tower and glided in on a long final, with one hand on the throttle and the other on the rip cord. All field traffic was clear, as everyone else had long since landed. I touched down on the numbers (there weren't any) right on the very end and rolled to a stop as the four huge Hamilton Standard blades came to a mournful stop. Strangely, I had run out of gas.

Number Thirteen was towed into our flight line to a welcoming throng of one mechanic who helped me down from the cockpit. To everyone else, it was just another F4U returning from a combat mission. To me, it was front-page news: I'd escaped prison camp, a near fatal shoot-out at the

The author, 1st Lt. D. K. Tooker, Korea, early 1951, poses beside his combat-loaded Corsair. For the Sinuiju air raid, the side number on Tooker's plane was thirteen.

"K-14 Corral," *and* a low-altitude bailout. At the very least, these had been defining moments.

The seventy-sixth mission was finished, as I nearly was. The wonderful self-sealing feature of the USA-made Corsair had saved my life and that of my aircraft. The semiliquid rubber-based material had slowly seeped into the jagged hole caused by the antiaircraft shrapnel and stemmed the flow of leaking gasoline just in time. Along with the knowledge that this wonderful technical innovation actually worked, I'd learned another important fact: I wasn't bulletproof, as I had previously believed. And although it was a close call, perhaps too close, combat for me remains the ultimate flying experience.

The aircraft was inspected and pronounced safe to fly home to K-3, which we'd left earlier the same day. My log book tells me that the self-sealing patch was so effective that I even flew Number Thirteen the next day, on my seventy-seventh mission. Shortly after that, the fuel cell was replaced, but the ship was later lost in combat. At least thirteen was a lucky number for me.

Epilogue

The results of the big mission were revealed several days later. Total bombing saturation had achieved the desired results. No attempt was ever made again to move aircraft into North Korea by the Chinese Communists.

Sadly, I failed to get my little brother safely through the war. Second Lt. J. J. Prior was killed in bad weather south of the bomb line on 10 July 1951. His plane was found with his body still in the cockpit. Why he'd failed to bail out was never learned. Majors Bob Stigall and Peter Van Ness, recently promoted, were killed at MCAS El Toro in August 1953, when their TV-2 (F-80) crashed on takeoff because of a complete engine failure. They were too low to bail out; low-altitude ejection seats were not yet available. I escorted the body of Robert Stigall home to St. Joseph, Missouri. He was my closest and dearest friend, and it was the hardest thing I had ever done. Lady Luck for some, like me, can be forgiving, but for others she taketh away.

7 Stand Well Clear

Marine Colonel Ken Reusser, who starred in three chapters of my first book, *The Second-Luckiest Pilot*, did not want me to write this story. He dragged his feet through every interview, would not dictate a tape, and was generally uncooperative in every aspect. He even took a year and a half to come up with the accompanying photographs.

To understand why he was so reticent about divulging the details of this story, you have to honor—as he did—the sensibilities of the nineteen-year-old that he was when he lived it. It wasn't as though he had anything to hide. After all, his Marine Corps career of some twenty-eight years had been more than successful. He flew combat missions in World War II and he won the Navy Cross, the nation's second highest award, for downing a Japanese aircraft with his propeller (his guns were frozen). Later, in Korea, he flew with me in combat (but received no special award for that particular accomplishment). He did, however, win his second Navy Cross for gallantry during this "police action." Finally in Vietnam, by then a full colonel, and while personally directing the recovery of a disabled CH-46 helicopter in enemy territory, he was shot down in a UH-1E chopper by the North Vietnamese. His copilot was killed instantly, and the two crewmen died in the ensuing fiery crash. Ken survived, but he was so badly burned that after months of recuperation he was retired with 100 percent disability. His decorations include two Navy Crosses, five Distinguished Flying Crosses, the Legion of Merit, and twelve Air Medals, to name only a few. In the combined three wars he'd flown more than two hundred combat missions.

But to say that this man never made a mistake while flying would be incorrect. My feeling is that you, the reader, have an inalienable right to know if Ken had ever screwed up (aviation talk). You are entitled to the facts, as long as you remember that his government was grateful enough to forgive him his imperfections and you probably should, too.

It was November of 1940. At nineteen, Ken wanted to become a naval aviator, at a time when the enigma of the United States entering into a war already in progress was on everyone's mind. Ken had looked into joining the British RAF and the Canadian RCAF. He had all the qualifications save one; he did not know how to fly—a somewhat necessary requirement. To fulfill it he had signed up for the Navy-sponsored civilian pilot training (CPT) program, which was available at small airports around the country. The airfield at Swan Lake, Oregon, offered this training and was located only a few miles from Ken's home in Portland. The purpose of the CPT program was to provide flight hours to prospective fliers who, if successful, would continue as aviation cadets in the formal naval flight training program. Thus, if the "almost cadet" couldn't handle the rigors of small light-plane flying, he would be dropped *before* the government spent the time and money only to learn that the wannabe pilot wasn't meant for the U.S. Navy's air arm.

Needless to say, Ken had no problem with flying the likes of Piper Cubs, Aeroncas, and Porterfields. He'd mastered the airborne maneuvers such as stalls, spin recoveries, mild aerobatics, and basic landing techniques such as S-turns to a circle, small field procedures, and simulated emergencies where the instructor would cut the throttle suddenly and say something like, "OK, engine failure. Pick a landing spot and let's see if you can put her down in one piece."

Ken was particularly proficient at this phase of training, and almost every time he would pick a satisfactory piece of real estate, where a landing could reasonably be expected to be one of the walk-away-from kind. Not to take anything away from this neophyte aviator, but there *were* two factors operating in his favor: (1) In 1940 most of Oregon was open fields; and (2) the landing speed of Piper Cubs and Porterfields was about thirty-five to thirty-eight miles per hour. If the student pilot was alert enough to plan his "emergency" approach and landing into the wind, which might average twelve to fifteen miles per hour, then the landing ground speed would only be around twenty-five miles per hour. At these breakneck speeds, simulated emergencies were rarely unsuccessful, and then only when the student froze at the controls. Ken never froze then, nor did he later in life, when he experienced actual emergencies in the F4U

Corsair—with average landing speeds approaching 100 mph.

Anyway, for our fledgling aviator the big day finally arrived, and every pilot, military and civilian, knows what this is. It is . . . the First Solo. It is a transformative event: In the morning, at breakfast, Ken was a student, under instruction. At lunch, after soloing, he was a *pilot*. Some say that, aside from sex, there is no better feeling than soloing. The reader can decide, but only if he or she has actually experienced both.

Be that as it may, even after a CPT student had achieved the right to fly alone around the Oregon countryside, his training continued. Usually the instructor would accompany his student on every third flight and monitor his progress as he gained more experience and, just as importantly, his confidence. The two flights between the dual-controls instruction served to build up the new pilot's flight time while he learned to think in the air and, of course on the ground.

Ground thinking comes into play when taxiing the aircraft, while parking, during preflight checking and refueling, and in all the other activities involved when the airplane is just sitting there. Among such mundane passages of ground thinking is the matter of chocking the plane. This is like setting the brakes on a car on a hill. Rope or chain tie-downs are also handy, as the wind can easily move a plane into an area where it may not be welcome. A comparable activity, in appropriately equipped aircraft, would be thinking about setting the parking brake. In a Porterfield, it must be noted, there was no parking brake to think about.

But back to the story. As Ken's total flight time grew to about thirty hours, so did his confidence. Perhaps, in retrospect, the latter outdistanced the former. The students were allowed, even encouraged, to take short cross-country flights, both to build up that all-important flight time and to teach the young pilot how to navigate by map and to perform landings at different airfields and grass strips. As noted, the relatively slow landing speeds of these small light aircraft meant that they could land almost anywhere—in a field, a road, even a pasture. Ken decided on a beautiful fall morning in 1940 that it was high time to show Uncle Elmer, his mother's brother, that he had more than mastered the fine art of piloting. His uncle owned a large ranch which was about forty-five miles southwest of the Swan Island airport. In those days most Oregon ranches were called farms, and Uncle Elmer raised cattle and hay on his 240-acre spread.

A telephone call (not even long distance then) revealed that his uncle would be more than delighted to see Ken and his new flying machine.

"I've got a pasture, just mowed, that runs right up to the barn," Elmer had reported, "and I'm pretty sure there's no big rocks there any more. What time would you be here?"

"About eleven o'clock," Ken replied. He was encouraged to hear that the big rocks were "pretty sure" not there anymore. "I'll have Carl with me in the front seat. He's come down from Portland to see the Porterfield. He's never been up before."

Ken was close to his younger brother, who had just turned sixteen. Carl wanted very much to fly as his older brother did, but he knew it might never happen; his vision was very poor, requiring some thick corrective lenses. Both brothers were extremely proud that Ken was almost through his initial phase of flight training and soon would be receiving orders for the next segment, Navy Preflight School.

Hillsboro Airport was a much larger aviation facility than Swan Island. It was home to a local FBO (fixed base operator) named Swede Ralston, who offered eight to ten aircraft for rent, one of which was a Porterfield, vintage 1939, similar to those in which Ken had received his training. After Ken had shown the owner his log book, replete with the carefully entered thirty hours, the paperwork and the aircraft rental agreement were in place. It had all the complexity of a quick handshake.

Ken's "I'll be back in a couple of hours," completed the negotiations.

As brother Carl followed closely behind, Ken carefully checked the aircraft explaining everything as they circled the plane a couple of times, once more than really necessary. With Carl strapped in securely in front by his safety belt, Ken settled himself in the back seat of the tandem aircraft. A mechanic who happened to be standing nearby agreed to prop-start the Porterfield when Ken would signal that he was ready. There were few electric starters in the early days of flying, and most small planes had to be propped by hand to start the engine. This was a particularly dangerous procedure and best performed by an experienced person.

"Switch off," Ken shouted. The mechanic then pulled the propeller through several times to prime the engine and drain any accumulated oil from the four cylinders.

"Switch on!" A short pause and then, "Clear!" This was said by the pilot to tell everyone to *stand well clear*. With the magnetos (two ignition switches) on, the assisting ground member then would pull the propeller downward with both hands and step quickly backward as the engine started.

After several attempts, the engine roared into life. A brief

How to start a 1939 Porterfield. Hand-propping expertly demonstrated. *Reusser collection*

warm-up and a mag check (ignition, again), and Ken was satisfied that the aircraft and he were ready to depart. With the engine instruments checked once again, Ken signaled to the mechanic by pointing both thumbs outward to pull the chocks. A quick thumbs-up by both the pilot and mechanic said, "Thanks for the help" and also "You're welcome." Some airplane talk is pretty basic.

Ken taxied out to the takeoff end of the grass strip, S-turning all the way so as to see ahead better. He had already noted the wind direction and would, just prior to departing, visually check for other aircraft in the landing pattern who would have the right of way. There was no control tower, and there were no radios aboard the Porterfield.

The takeoff was routine, and Ken headed to the west with his map carefully placed within easy reach. He'd already decided which highway he'd follow but felt more comfortable with the map, just in case of getting disoriented (pilots try not to use the word "lost"). Airborne communications were accomplished simply by shouting. Ken pointed out significant landmarks to Carl, such as the city of Portland and the two rather prominent rivers, the Willamette and the Columbia. They also passed over a white farm house that happened to be the home of a girlfriend. (She'd left Oregon to attend college in Colorado. This is interesting only in that she later became Ken's wife.)

Passing the heavily wooded hills south of Beaverton, they were soon over the neatly laid-out farms that from the air resembled a partially completed jigsaw puzzle.

"How do you like flying, Carl?" His answer was an emphatic nod from his position up front. Ken thought perhaps on the return flight he'd let him handle the controls to get a better feel of flying, after a brief explanation of what the stick and rudder functions were.

Uncle Elmer's 240 acres were easy to spot, as they were situated in a large saddle back between two smooth-looking hills with a fairly good-sized lake not far from the barn. They could see cattle grazing in several fenced-in areas. It was picture-postcard lovely and had been in the Reusser family for three generations.

The Porterfield responded perfectly as the two stalwarts circled the big barn and farmhouse to announce their arrival beyond any doubt. Uncle Elmer had apparently invited more than his immediate family, as there appeared from the rear cockpit to be at least twenty-five to thirty people gathered to see the Ken Reusser "air show."

The star performer flew slowly over the pasture, looking

for anything that might mar his landing rollout, such as those large rocks mentioned earlier by his uncle. They saw none, and the touchdown was perfect. Taxiing in, Ken knew immediately how Amelia Earhart must have felt after setting one of her many transcontinental records.

Ken proceeded carefully toward a barbed-wire fence near the big barn and shut off the mags. He got out first and then helped out brother Carl. No one moved to come closer to the aircraft. "Maybe they think it's going to explode," Ken thought. Then he realized that few of them had ever seen an airplane up close, much less flown in one. In 1940 not many adults from Oregon farms were aviation buffs.

Hugs, handshakes, and smiles abounded. Uncle Elmer introduced everyone, kids included, to "my nephew, the pilot." The word "proud" didn't come close to describing how Uncle Elmer felt. Everyone toured the Porterfield and carefully peered inside the cockpit at the incredible maze of instruments (all six of them). Most viewers also commented on how small the seating arrangements were. A pleasant hour ensued, and Ken then passed the word that he and Carl must begin their flight back to the Hillsboro airport. The spectators respectfully retreated to a more-than-safe distance to observe the start-up and departure proceedings.

It was at this point that Ken suddenly realized something he had not thought of before. There was no one around who was qualified to prop-start the aircraft. And he was certainly not about to ask any of the local observers to perform this somewhat dangerous task of spinning the propeller. He himself would have to handle those duties. He remembered reading about and talking with some old-timers who often traveled alone around the country. They would start their engines by carefully chocking the wheels, then setting the throttle and switches in the cockpit, swinging the propeller; and as soon as the engine caught, running quickly around the wing and climbing into the cockpit. Once the engine was warmed up, they would rev the engine with enough power to jump over the chocks, which were usually rocks chosen to be just the right size. It sounded a little crazy to Ken when he first heard about using rocks for chocks, but he knew it was not uncommon—at least *then*. Of course, a good reliable parking brake pretty much solved this problem later on. He remembered again that the Porterfield had no such luxury.

With little else in the offing, he'd decided on his course of action. He had one big advantage over being alone—his brother Carl. Ken would set the switches and crack the throttle, and he would swing the wooden propeller to start the engine. A quick search located two rocks that seemed just made for their important mission. He placed them carefully in front of the sausagelike wheels, checked all switches "off" and pulled the prop through several times to prime the engine. He returned to the cockpit, opening the throttle just a crack, and pushed in both magnetos. His plan of departure was to warm up the engine, add enough power to jump over the rocks, taxi back down to the pasture takeoff area, and, once airborne, fly by and "dip a wing," as per his uncle's request. Things didn't work out quite that way.

Ken's briefing to his brother, seated in the front seat, was Wiley Post simple: "Don't touch anything. Just wait for me to get back inside, OK?" The old affirmative nod again.

After waving goodbye several times to the onlookers, Ken swung the prop down smartly. The engine only coughed. The second try was successful. As Ken stepped back from the spinning propeller, an unplanned event occurred. Brother Carl, upon hearing the engine backfire slightly as it started, became startled and instinctively, at least for him, reached forward for a better grip on something—anything. In so doing, his arm or elbow hit the throttle forward to the full open position. The engine, being cold, hesitated momentarily, just long enough for Ken to duck under the right wing and grab onto the wing strut. As he did so, the engine roared into its full power condition, dragging a bouncing Ken along the ground toward the fence less than a hundred feet away. He shouted to Carl to close the throttle—to no avail. He was frozen, mesmerized by the startling chain of events. As the aircraft gathered forward speed, the nose lifted as the engine's momentum increased. Ken had a death grip with his right hand on the wing strut. Suddenly, he was lifted off the ground and swung toward the open cockpit door.

Desperately, he threw his left arm into the cockpit, somehow managing to hit the throttle lever, moving it aft to the idle position. As the aircraft reluctantly settled back to earth, the engine, now almost powerless, was no longer in command. Ken killed the switches and then took stock of the situation. His brother was still staring straight ahead, as if looking elsewhere would further implicate him as a wrongdoer. The spectators, needless to say, were standing motionless, slack-jawed.

The lightplane was injured, although Ken and his brother were not. During its brief leap for freedom, the aircraft had unfortunately come down upon one of the six-foot fence posts nearby. Its right wing was impaled on the post, strongly suggesting a layer cake with one lone candle sticking out of the middle.

The family and friends prudently continued their silent vigil while Ken made his inspection of the damage. It was excellent luck that no barbed wire remained attached to the fence post. They had just the post to deal with. After a lengthy discussion with his uncle and one of his neighbors, they decided to enlist all hands present in lifting the airplane up and off the post.

"Then we can see how much damage there is," the neighbor had suggested. Ken wondered how many lightplanes the neighbor had seen previously, to be such an authority on what to do with an aircraft that had a fence pole stuck through its wing. Whatever his background, the neighbor was right.

Lifting the little plane up and off the post with the muscle of a dozen or so of the onlookers proved to be no problem. Ken was glad he wasn't flying a heavier, metal-covered, twin-engine aircraft. The inspection by Ken, his uncle, and the knowledgeable neighbor, once the plane had been pushed to a "safe" area way from the fence post, revealed no damage to the main wing spar. Only the fabric on the top and bottom of the wing was punctured and torn. It looked much worse than it actually was. This, however, did not assuage Ken's embarrassment, as he realized how terribly serious things could have been.

"It can't fly like this," he said aloud, to himself. One of the helpers overheard him and added his own touch of gloom. "Had a brother that flew. World War I. Jennys, I think they said they was. Ran out of gas one night."

Ken looked around at him inquiringly. The neighbor finished the story. "Killed in thirty-two. Haven't ever gone up in one myself."

"Oh," Ken responded, thoughtfully. This was no time to convert anybody to the joys of flight, and his mind was spinning, propeller-fashion, toward a solution to his dilemma. But then Uncle Elmer came over to him with a suggestion.

"Why can't we just tape her up, you know, like a patch?"

Why not, indeed? No one had a better idea, least of all Ken. "I've got some adhesive tape I'm pretty sure. I'll go look." With that Uncle Elmer ambled off and returned shortly with enough tape to bandage all the wounded at Gettysburg.

Fortunately, the rather substantial holes were inboard of the ailerons, which for obvious reasons could not be taped immobile. Using a small stepladder, the uncle and the neighbor (whose name Ken never learned) proceeded to wrap the right wing with four-inch adhesive tape, around and around. It looked, when they finished, much like a human being taped for a cracked rib. The bright yellow wing, now with a white ring around it, made an interesting picture. After a final and careful inspection by Ken, the historic return flight was rescheduled.

Again, good-byes all around, this time in a more somber mood. Ken chocked the wheels with the same rocks as before but only after facing the Porterfield away from the obtrusive fence post. He pulled the propeller through four revolutions, turned the switches on, and cracked the throttle open slightly. Before beginning the hand-propping procedure, he'd suggested quietly to his brother that it might be better if he would just stand by one of the wing tips until everything was "settled down," as Ken thoughtfully put it. "Then you can get in." Carl was in complete agreement.

The engine caught on the first swing of the propeller

Swede and Ken with the storied Porterfield, sixty-one years later. Its current owner hangars it at Swede's fixed base operation.
Reusser collection

and the two travelers strapped in. With a final wave to the observers, Ken added power and the aircraft hopped over the two rocks without incident. As he taxied down toward the takeoff end of the pasture, Ken decided that after becoming airborne there would be no dipping the wing as his uncle had requested. Instead he'd head straight home to face the music, whatever that might be. He'd had enough excitement for one day.

They landed at the Hillsboro airport and taxied over to the tie-down area. Several onlookers stared intently at the newly decorated wing. Ken shut down the engine after telling his brother not to worry and sent him home right away. Carl was never heard to complain, after that, that his poor eyesight denied him a career as a pilot.

Swede Ralston, the owner of the 1939 aircraft, was very matter-of-fact about his damaged Porterfield. Ken had related the incident truthfully, in a straightforward manner. After inspecting the bandaged wing and removing the two or three miles of adhesive tape, the FBO operator concurred with the earlier findings at Uncle Elmer's farm.

"Doesn't seem to be any obvious damage to the main wing spar," the Swede had said. "We'll have to recover most of the wing fabric. Would you be willing to pay for that?" Ken was only too glad to comply.

"I don't think the damage here is enough to bother the CPT guys with, do you?"

"No Sir, I wouldn't think so," Ken readily agreed. An incident like this could throw a serious wrench into the works, the U.S. Navy not always being so understanding in the area of aircraft accidents.

"What can you pay, Ken? I know you're going to college. Could you handle twenty dollars a month? I figure it'll run around $200 or so to do the job correctly."

"Yes Sir. I'll send you a money order every month. I do some manual labor over in Portland." Ken paused. "I really appreciate your understanding on this, Mr. Ralston."

"That's OK. I wish you luck and hope you make it through your navy flight-training program."

For six straight months Ken dutifully sent a money order for the $20 repayment. The following month he received orders to a naval preflight school in Seattle, Washington, and his letter to the FBO owner was so postmarked. A week later in the return mail he got a note from Swede, saying: "The bill for the repairs of the Porterfield has been fully taken care of. Thank you for your honesty and best of luck in your new career." He couldn't have known just how successful a career the future Marine colonel would have, or how that honesty would translate into gallantry in action thousands of miles from his Uncle Elmer's farm.

Epilogue

Mr. Swede Ralston is alive and well as of this writing and comes to the Portland-Hillsboro Airport several times a week to oversee his fixed base operation, Aero Air, where he is well known in Oregon as an aviation pioneer. He is almost eighty-seven years old, and he and Ken still stay in touch, but neither one flies the Porterfield anymore.

8 First Flight of Second Lieutenant Sprague

The fifth of May, 1956, held no particular significance for the marines stationed at Quantico, Virginia, on that date, unless they happened to have guests from Mexico who wanted to celebrate Cinco de Mayo. It was just another Sunday.

On this particular spring Sunday morning, however, three highly motivated, clear-eyed Marine pilots sitting at their breakfast table at Camp Upshur, one of the outlying locations where young marine officer candidates were taught the rudiments of officerhood, were discussing a problem.

These three pilots had completed their training in the Naval Flight Training Program but had not been through either Marine boot camp or TBS ("The Basic School"). The latter was designed to indoctrinate college graduates on the niceties of becoming a Marine officer. It was a six-month program, but these young aviators were expected to complete it in six weeks.

Getting through all the subjects in TBS took all their weekday and Saturday hours. But they also had to fly four hours a month if they wanted to earn their flight pay and maintain a required level of proficiency. So Sundays, their only day off, was often dedicated to getting airborne.

This Cinco de Mayo was such a Sunday, and the three elite and select (in their minds) pilots had a problem—a basic lack of vehicular transportation. The airfield at Quantico was perhaps eighteen to twenty miles away, and none of the three had a car. In those days Marine families rarely owned two cars, so the wife retained possession while her spouse went off to war or "school"—in this case lovely Camp Upshur.

All three marines were captains and friends from previous duty stations. From left to right they were Vic Gouty, Mike Mura, and T. R. Moore. With breakfast they chewed their toast along with the logistic problem of procuring a round-trip ride to the air station. Captain Mura had an idea: "Maybe one of the Basic School guys would like to go flying. Particularly one with a car."

This idea met with enthusiastic approval, and the pilots began a carefully orchestrated (not too eager, not too diffi-dent) search for someone, anyone, who might like to go fly-ing, *and* owned a car.

T. R. Moore made the find. After carefully describing the boundless joys of flight and the high untrespassed sanctity of space, and not forgetting that they would be slipping the surly bonds of earth, he won a volunteer: One 2d Lt. Paul B. Sprague agreed to the plan. His car would hold all four gen-tlemen, and the deal was struck.

Captain Moore became the spokesman/leader and laid out the plan of flight in the car as the young lieutenant carefully navigated through the Quantico speed zones. He also observed all caution signs. Second lieutenants almost always do this. He may or may not have been listening while Moore was outlining their flight plan.

"I'd say we take off and head southwest of Quantico, away from the river"—the Potomac—"and work in the free-flight maneuver area. We'd be clear of all the airways then." As they rode along, Moore was already mentally aloft. "We can do some formation flying, maybe a tail-chase and then come back and shoot some touch-and-goes." The other two pilots were in complete agreement.

Captain Gouty spoke: "I haven't flown the SNJ for awhile. Guess it'll come back to me."

"It will," Captain Mura said. "If you can start it, you can fly it."

He was pretty much on track. The SNJ, or AT-6 in the USAF, was a tandem two-seated trainer commonly called the "Texan." It was and still is known to be a reliable flight trainer and was even rugged enough to fly aboard carriers in the mid to late forties.

T. R. spoke: "You guys are going to scare our vehicle operator, talking like that. He should be aware that we all have hundreds of hours of flying experience and have had no pilot-caused accidents. Right?" A brief silence was followed by the nodding of heads in concurrence.

If Lieutenant Sprague was apprehensive, he did not show it. In truth, he never had flown before, nor had he even sat in an airplane. The farthest off the ground he'd been was the top of the Washington Monument, and that was the previous weekend. He had climbed many steps to get there. He'd heard, "Marines don't take the elevator."

On the ride out to the airfield Moore had regaled the group about his only accident, that of backing a plowing tractor through both sides of a barn because he couldn't get it out of reverse. "Scared the chickens near to death and they didn't lay for almost a week." Whether totally true or not, it was a great story and received top billing from the other passengers. T. R., as he was called by everyone, always had his sense of humor idling in the background, ready for action. Besides being a superb pilot, he also had a talent for convincing the less gifted that the earth really was flat or that his way was the only way. On the job, his preflight briefings were always thorough, but lightened with humor—mostly common sense with a little nonsense mixed in.

The weather was clear. The three SNJ's were parked in the ready position and the required flight plan filed with Operations. The three pilots had changed into flight gear from their lockers in the hangar; Lieutenant Sprague wore his summer service khaki uniform. For all four, helmets and parachutes had been checked out from the paraloft, and the proverbial, "Let's get 'em into the air," had been announced by Captain Gouty.

T. R. reconfirmed the general flight plan with both Gouty and Mura. The three were to rendezvous over nearby Fredericksburg at five thousand feet, left-hand orbit.

Lieutenant Sprague had listened very intently as T. R. went over their flight intentions and how to buckle in—shoulder straps, seat belt, and so on.

"Paul, in the very unlikely event we should ever have to bail out, here is what you do: On my word, and only on *my* word, you'll dive over the left side of the aircraft. Remember to disconnect the radio cord from your hard hat"—helmet—"undo your safety belt, and then aim for the trailing edge of the wing. The slipstream will make you miss it. Do not, repeat *do not*, pull the rip cord, yes, that's the 'D' ring over your heart, until you're clear of the aircraft. OK? You got that?"

"Yes, Sir," was the rather quiet response. "Have you ever had to jump, Captain?"

"No, Paul, never. But I wanted you to be briefed just in case. It's like the FAA requirement on the airlines about that little oxygen mask that will automatically drop down in the unlikely event of a loss in cabin pressure." The lieutenant merely nodded. He hadn't the vaguest idea of what the captain was talking about, having never been in any airplane before, and no such announcements had been made when he'd climbed the Washington Monument. He did feel entirely confident that his parachute briefing had been accurate and complete.

T. R. had been particularly conscientious in presenting the emergency bail-out instructions, because he had recently read, in a military publication, about an incident in Oahu, Hawaii, where an air force pilot in an AT-6 had an engine failure over the Pali mountain range and his passenger, when ordered to jump, froze and refused to bail out no matter what the pilot said to him. The pilot finally jumped, but the panicked passenger rode it in and was killed. Stories like that stick in the mind.

The three aircraft were directed by the tower to use runway 18 for takeoff to the south with T. R. and his passenger in the lead SNJ. Gouty and Mura followed as solo-piloted aircraft.

The flight proceeded as planned, with some formation flying immediately after their rendezvous. Each pilot took his turn as the flight leader for around half an hour at a time. Next, a mild tail chase was performed, with the three aircraft in close-column formation as the pilots enjoyed the pleasures of relaxed flying. The sky was clear, the scenery beautiful and the air smooth as silk. T. R. radioed the others that he thought he could see all the way to St. Louis. His passenger in the back seat smiled at this and in fact already had assured his pilot that he was not experiencing any air sickness. He'd radioed through the intercom, "Sir, this is really great!"

"Baker Flight from Leader. Let's break up and do some individual air work. I'm going back and shoot some touch-and-goes, and I think one of us ought to go down and check out the roof of that girls' college in Fredericksburg for any nude sunbathers—gettin' to be that time of year." It is unlikely that Marymount College ever supplied nude bathers to be spotted from the air, but the possibility sounded pretty macho over the VHF channel. T. R.'s passenger undoubtedly figured that pilots really do have a good deal, the lucky bastards.

"OK, Paul, we're going to do a split-S now. We're at seven thousand feet and it's the quickest way to lose altitude. We'll pull out around twenty-five hundred feet. Tighten your shoulder straps." So saying, T. R. rolled the aircraft to an inverted position and let the nose drop through until they were pointed straight down. Even though he'd reduced throttle, the speed built up rapidly.

As the plane sped earthward, the rpm suddenly went crazy. The propeller oversped, almost instantly exceeding the red-line maximum marked on the instrument. T. R. knew at once that the propeller governor had either failed or malfunctioned. He closed the throttle and pulled back on the stick with all his strength, nearly blacking out from the

G forces, as this was the only way to regain manageable propeller rpm. When they leveled off, the engine began to vibrate and then miss. Glancing at the altimeter, which read twenty-six hundred feet, T. R. immediately switched to tower frequency.

"Quantico Tower, this is Marine Four One Baker, fifteen miles south with a rough runner. Request a straight-in to runway three six." The response was immediate.

"Roger, Four One Baker. You're cleared straight in as requested. Will clear all traffic. Advise when you have the field in sight."

"Roger that, Tower. Understand cleared straight in," he'd responded as he searched the cockpit instruments for some answers. He remembered his passenger suddenly and said:

"Don't worry, Paul. We'll get her back, but you can be looking for a vacant lot or two." There was no response from the back seat.

The terrain below, so beautiful moments ago, was now totally unforgiving—ninety-foot jack pines, unyielding to SNJ trainers or for that matter to any airplane. They were too far west for the familiar pattern of roads that ran along the shores of the Potomac. Now twenty-three hundred feet registered on the altimeter. With the terrain level at three hundred feet, that meant an actual two thousand feet above the ground, T. R. remembered. The engine was missing badly, and the cylinder head temperature had pegged.

"You still holding up, Paul?"

"Yes, Sir." His voice was surprisingly calm, with only a hint of tension in it.

"I'm not seeing those vacant lots yet," T. R. said, trying to sound matter-of-fact. As he released the transmitting button on the intercom, the game entered a new phase of seriousness. The engine seized and the propeller froze in the twelve o'clock position, and T. R. could read what every pilot fears reading: the manufacturer's name on the prop—in this case, HAMILTON STANDARD.

"Paul, we're running out of ideas and altitude. We're going to have to bail out. You go first while I hold it straight and level. Let's go! We don't have much time." No acknowledgment from the back seat. T. R. turned to look behind him and saw two saucerlike eyes staring at him. He remembered the passenger in Hawaii.

"Paul! Bail out or you'll die!!" That did it. The Basic School passenger suddenly disappeared over the left side of the aircraft, his radio cord pulling off his helmet, which he'd forgotten to disconnect. But he'd done everything else correctly and had avoided hitting the empennage (the tail surfaces).

Glancing for one final look at the altimeter, which told him he was really too low to bail out, T. R. yanked the radio cord loose and dove out the left side of the cockpit. He'd pulled his rip cord immediately, heedless of the risk of striking the elevator with his body. After what seemed to be many seconds of nothing, there was a violent jerk as the chute deployed. He swung once, feet high above his head, like a clock's pendulum and then hit the ground like a sack of ball bearings (his words) flat on his back.

After regaining both his composure and the wind that had been knocked out of him, he took stock of the situation. He'd landed in a small clearing, apparently the only one around. His chute had one torn panel, which possibly could explain why he'd hit so hard. Next, he inventoried his extremities. All were present and accounted for, and he found no apparent broken bones. His back hurt like hell, because he'd landed on it rather than on his feet, as recommended in most parachutists' manuals. He would have corrective surgery for this trauma some six years later.

As he gathered up the chute, somewhat painfully, he noticed a heavily bearded man in his middle thirties, dressed in coveralls, approaching. He fulfilled T. R.'s mental picture of a local farmer.

"Boy, that first step's a humdinger, ain't it?" T. R. could not believe his ears. *Some hayseed thinks so little of my near-death experience that he'd crack the corniest of all jokes.* But his anger, and it was surfacing, turned to astonishment as the "hayseed" proceeded to explain that he'd been in the 101st Airborne Regiment in World War II and that he had made three combat jumps, the last one behind enemy lines during the Normandy Invasion. He even had a regimental shoulder patch sewn on his denim overalls to prove it.

"You don't look none the worse for wear," the farmer/paratrooper said. "Are you OK? Do you need a doctor?" he went on. "I heard an explosion a few minutes ago over near the McBerny place. Must have been your bird." T. R. nodded in agreement.

"You have a phone at your place?"

"Yes, I do. My name's Charlie. I made staff sergeant before I got out of the army," he added. With the formal introductions out of the way, the two chutists made their way up a slight rise toward a rather run-down farmhouse. Ever observant, T. R. noted that it needed painting. As they made their way toward it, Charlie confirmed T. R.'s surmise that he'd landed in the only clearing for miles. If he had missed it—

well, it didn't take much imagination to know how unfortunate it could be to come down in dense pine forest.

Having learned his location from Charlie, Captain Moore called in to report that he was safe and basically undamaged, that his aircraft had crashed nearby and was undoubtedly destroyed, and that his passenger also had bailed out but his whereabouts and condition were unknown.

As he was completing his call to the military authorities, people began arriving in cars, on bicycles, and on foot. The SNJ had apparently crashed only a few hundred yards down the country dirt road. In T. R.'s words, "They were coming out of the woodwork, some twenty-five or thirty of them, and pretty soon a guy in an ice cream truck shows up and starts selling ice cream bars—probably his best Sunday afternoon ever."

Charlie, who apparently lived alone, viewed the gawkers with scorn. He and T. R. returned to the clearing where they spread the parachute out on the ground. With several large rocks placed carefully to hold it down, the orange and white paneled nylon would serve as a recognition panel for the rescue helicopter coming from the Quantico Marine Base.

In about twenty minutes they heard the welcoming sound of the rotor blades of the rescue chopper. T. R. "popped" an orange smoke flare, much to the crowd's delight, to assist the helo pilot in assessing the wind direction. He didn't forget to shake hands with Charlie and to express his thanks for the fine hospitality. Now they both were candidates for the famed Caterpillar Club membership, the organization that "successful" parachute jumpers may join. For aviators, it should be stated, this is not always a desirable membership. In a few seconds Captain Moore was safely aboard the helicopter and headed for the mandatory medical inspection and debriefing.

T. R. Moore, ready to fly the SNJ Texan.
Someday he might need that parachute.
Moore collection

Seconds later he was pleased to greet Lieutenant Sprague, already aboard; he'd been picked up a few minutes earlier, only about two miles from where T. R. had landed at Charlie's place. But the lieutenant's experience was a different story altogether.

It seems that the young "bailoutee" had landed in one very tall pine tree in a heavily wooded area and somehow (the lieutenant didn't know how) ended up hanging upside down in his parachute harness some fifty feet above the ground. Terrified, initially, he was afraid to move for fear of falling headfirst from the equivalent height of a five-story building. His plaintive cries for help went unheard. Eventually, he built up his nerve and began, very tentatively at first, to swing in pendulumlike arcs, reaching out at the high point of his swings to grab a substantial part of the pine tree. Finally he was able to grasp a strong enough limb, unbuckle his parachute harness—as he explained, "ever so carefully"—and shinny down the tree to terra firma, grateful to be alive and glad that his landing was one he could walk away from. Lieutenant Sprague's first step had indeed been a "humdinger."

The chopper pilot had seen Sprague's parachute hanging in the pine tree. It was no problem to retrieve him from a small clearing nearby, by the time the shaken lieutenant had walked there.

Lieutenant Sprague enjoyed the second flight of his life considerably more than the first. He had only a few scratches from the pine branches but a large golf ball–sized lump on his forehead where he'd tangled, head-on, with the trunk. He remembered that he'd forgotten to unplug his radio cord and this little infraction—which had cost him his helmet— explained the now swelling bump on his head. But in both rescued pilots' minds, the paramount thought was something like: "Boy, am I glad to get through *that* one!"

Epilogue

The investigation revealed a malfunctioning propeller governor and confirmed that Captain Moore had made all the right decisions. It was not a pilot-caused accident, so the wayward tractor-barn demolishing incident remained T. R.'s only mishap of that kind. Lieutenant Sprague, as might be expected, became somewhat of a celebrity at Camp Upshur, wearing his injury rather proudly.

The downside of all this was immediately apparent: There were no further volunteers from the ground officers at the camp to exchange car rides for airplane rides.

9 The Pilots' Best Friend

This is a story about a car—not just any old car but a very old and special car—and the role it played in enhancing the social lives of some young fighter pilots. Stationed at an outlying field near Jacksonville, Florida, these pilots were sadly without wheels. They had no practical means of checking out the big city's lights or the attractions on nearby Jax Beach. The interests along this popular stretch of sand were not of the maritime nature. Yes, it was the girls, of which there was no wartime shortage. Hence, the desperate need for suitable transportation.

It was the middle of May, 1947, and the pilots, three U.S. Navy and one USMC, had just received their wings and commissions at Pensacola, Florida. They were now stationed at NAS (Naval Air Station) Cecil Field, located about thirty-five miles outside of Jacksonville. It was their immediate duty and privilege to learn how to make the transition from the 550-horsepowered SNJ Texan Trainer (T-6 in the air force) to the famous World War II F4U Corsair. The latter single-seat aircraft had almost five times the horsepower of the SNJ.

The Corsair had acquired a bad reputation in 1942 and early 1943. It had earned the nickname of "Ensign Eliminator," and because of its high fatality rate it was taken off the navy's carriers and "given" to the Marines. The tremendous torque developed by the huge Pratt & Whitney radial engine could cause the pilot to spin in on a last-minute wave-off, particularly on a carrier approach. The problem was eventually solved, and the Corsair became well known in the South Pacific in combat against the Japanese.

Now that the capsulated Corsair history lesson is over, let us return to the mission at hand: that of checking out in the F4U "U-Bird" at Cecil Field. Getting acquainted with the Corsair meant, first, a week of concentrated ground school, every day, all day, of being told, "Don't be afraid of this aircraft!" By the end of the week, of course, everyone *was* afraid of the aircraft. The cautionary drill was not intended to scare the daylights out of us, but neither were those briefings given to kamikaze pilots. That hellish week, designed to cultivate attention to and respect for the bentwing aircraft, primed us for a love-hate relationship with it. (That was the effect on me, even after a thousand hours and 130-plus combat missions, and I was not alone in that.)

But this is a story about an old car and its operators, not about the Corsair. As anyone who flies knows, there is almost always some tension, a degree of concern, you might say, associated with flying. And for the Corsair trainees, the answer to "What, me worry?" was, privately, "Yes!"—after

The beachgoers at work: Corsairs aloft, weekdays.

hearing for a solid week how dangerous this next step would be while moving up the operational performance ladder.

So what does the young neophyte pilot do about all that tension? Obviously, he goes to happy hour at the "O" Club, where he shoots the bull with the other soon-to-be high-performance aviators. No one admits to being scared of his forthcoming first flight in the navy's fastest and most dangerous fighter. But even the bartender can easily detect an air of "concern" from his patrons.

Lt. (jg) Paul Hayek, USN, acted as spokesman and shield bearer. He'd gone through his flight training as an officer, not as a cadet as had the other three pilots. He had served three years on a heavy cruiser during the war in the "black shoe" navy and had opted for the flying part of the naval service at his earliest opportunity, in his words. Thus, he was the "old man" at twenty-three in our group of four.

Paul opened the discussion one night at the "O" Club

during this first week of indoctrination as the pilots drank their cold bottles of beer, right out of the neck.

"As I see it," he began, "we are in somewhat need of diversionment." Paul had a way with words, even if they weren't in Mr. Webster's big best seller.

"That's for sure," Buddy Rich agreed. Bud was an ensign, as was Al Fox. D. K. Tooker rounded out the quartet as the only marine, a dashing second lieutenant.

"But we need to get to town." Al voiced the unspoken challenge on all our minds. "And we can't do that without a car." We all nodded in agreement. "The station buses run less often than Halley's Comet." Unhappily, in this, too, he was correct, if only in strength of metaphor rather than astronomical accuracy. As despair descended on us, Paul resumed command.

"There's not much available in the used car market, and production of new stuff hasn't caught up with demand. World wars can do that, you realize. But we need to get a car."

"Perhaps we should send out a posse and scout downtown Jacksonville," Bud suggested. "I'll volunteer if someone will go with me. Tomorrow's Saturday."

Paul was elected by self-acclamation to complete the car-buying team. Neither of the two "selectees" had ever owned a car. In truth, none of the four pilots had. A price limit, easily agreed upon, for the big purchase was determined by whoever could produce the least amount of cash. Paul held higher rank than the others and made more money, but his maximum input was $150. He blamed being poor on the market conditions; the others knew he meant supermarkets. Finally six hundred big ones were amassed, and the venture was on.

Another marine, one Jim Rice, who happened to overhear the clandestine car plotting, offered to take the investors to town the next morning in his blue 1941 Chevrolet. The offer was quickly accepted from the man who had everything: good looks, money (he was a captain), *and* a car.

That Saturday evening was a not-to-be-forgotten occasion. The two "car experts" did not bring back a load of girls to their lonely desert outpost, but they did drive up, with the horn blowing, in a car big enough to comfortably seat all four new car owners. But even better, there was plenty of extra seating for possible female riders, should the new car owners be fortunate enough to coerce said ladies into the newly acquired chariot.

The car was as huge as it was old. It was a 1924 Detroit Paige, with running boards a foot and a half wide, two jump seats in the back, and two huge spare tires nestled on each side of the engine hood. It had a large trunk rack in the rear, which could (and did) support two wooden, tin-lined .50-caliber ammunition boxes for beer. Every pilot knows that the cubic footage of two ammo boxes accommodates two cases of beer, with plenty of room for ice.

The car was a bilious olive green and was promptly named "The Blue Blooper." Part of the new name was explainable: As the motor was started and began running well, the slightly defective muffler emitted a different sound from that of other four-cylinder engines. It was like a "bloop" noise, sort of a popping sound but deeper. Attempts to describe it proved fruitless; you just had to be there.

The seller, a retired night watchman in Jacksonville, had kept the antique vehicle on blocks in his garage for nearly twenty years. He hadn't said why, and the car buyers had not asked. The former watchman had asked $1,000 for the car but lowered his price when Paul and Bud convinced him there was only $600 in the kitty.

Everything on the car was original, the wheels (not the tires), the upholstery, even the tubular driver-to-passenger telephone. However, a twelve-volt electrical system had replaced the original six-volt one, enabling the headlights to function reasonably well. The brakes were another story. They were absolutely original, and that was the problem. They were of the two-wheel variety, as opposed to the four-wheel type. It soon became apparent that about two city blocks were needed to stop the behemoth once it had achieved full speed, anywhere around forty-five to fifty miles per hour.

The Blue Blooper's braking feature, or the lack thereof, promptly brought about the unintentional running of a stop sign on the base in front of the building that housed the military police. This event, in turn inspired a brilliant strategy whereby a "brake person" was assigned to sit next to the driver; upon the command, "Brakes!" he (or she) would grab the emergency brake lever. This engaged the separate mechanical brake shoes and added another fifty percent to the stopping capability of the Blooper. The 2,000-pound vehicle could now stop in a much shorter distance—one Texas block.

This braking individual could be a lady person if she were so inclined to accept this position of responsibility. The resulting seating arrangement met with enthusiastic approval from the pilot group, as it meant boy-girl, boy-girl seat assignments. It turned out that these female copilots took to their role quite enthusiastically, perhaps because of the chances of being asked to attend an "O" Club gala event, not to mention the continually scheduled beach parties.

For that kind of mission the Blue Blooper excelled, capably conveying its passengers along the wide and hard-packed sands of the popular and nearby Jax Beach. What with warm weather and warm water, coupled with cold beer, the big car soon became the focal point of many beach parties, even those that were unscheduled. An observer mounted on the vehicle's roof in a four-man rubber raft, scanning the horizon with two empty beer bottles, was a signal of imminent festivities to all beholders. Whenever a bevy of lady beachgoers was sighted, the pilots inside the car leaned out and called loud and clear: "Beach Party just south of the pier in thirty minutes; free beer. Y'all come." And they did.

The pilots were unique in that they had a car that everyone, guys included (although they were not quite as welcome as girls), wanted to know more about. The jump seats were points of interest, as were the wooden spoked wheels, which creaked loudly when the car was in motion.

Bud Rich, whose real first name was Wallace, went on in his career to become a member of the U.S. Navy's famed Blue Angels from 1952 to 1954. In 1947, however, he put the girl scouting (so to speak) in perspective when he said, "Back in Santa Cruz where I grew up, the best way to meet a pretty girl on the beach was to bring a young puppy with you. No gal could resist a warm cuddly puppy." All hands agreed. So the pilots had improvised a tad and had employed a warm, cuddly eight-passenger, twenty-three-year-old car. The final consensus put the car way ahead of the puppy ploy, and besides, the car wouldn't wet on your beach towel.

With such charm, good looks (the pilots' viewpoint) and a great automobile, the group pretty much had the pick of the litter. They had it made and they knew it. To even better their good fortune, a volunteer "duty driver" was located (another pilot). He was assigned his nondrinking driver duties to ensure vehicular safety and to keep the partying members of the group out of jail. This duty man was efficient, good-natured, and much in demand. He had been properly instructed as to the little problem of stopping the Blooper in reasonably short distances.

In short, the elite group had the best of both worlds: an exciting life flying the fastest prop fighter in the world during the week and exercising their beach-partying rights on the weekends, in style.

All great days at the beach must end, of course, and driving the party car back to the base on Sunday evenings was often something of an adventure. On one occasion, a heavy tropical Florida rain had forced an early shutting down of all beach festivities, although the party continued from inside the big car. Pleasant and sociable sounds rose above the rumble of its engine. Libations flowed, as did the fantastic aviation sea stories. The duty driver informed the merry group that he, along with the car, was heading for the air station. Heavy weather was closing in, and he was afraid of the dark—as any sane person driving a car with virtually no headlights or brakes reasonably would be. (His concerns—those thought processes that we reserved for aviation—were resolutely ignored).

Once the girls were dropped off, the car assumed the correct heading for its home base. The brake person, Bud Rich, took up his position of responsibility as the rain came down in buckets. Forward visibility was down to about forty or fifty feet on the narrow two-lane road. Approximately ten miles from the warmth of the main gate, a cow suddenly appeared directly ahead.

"Brakes!" the duty driver ordered. Even at thirty miles an hour it was no use. The right front of the car rendezvoused with the poor cow, sending her flying into the flooded grass ditch at the side of the road. The two-thousand-pound vehicle then backed up as the pilots leaped out into the downpour to inspect the damage to both parties. Al Fox was the first to reach the animal.

"I think she's had it, guys. She's not breathing, as far as I can tell." His medical opinion was, to everyone's dismay, correct. Paul spoke next.

"The fender and the bumper are OK. The spring steel bumper must have taken most of the shock; in fact, the fender only has a slight crease. Christ, I remember when my dad hit a deer once, wiped out the whole front of the car."

"So, now what do we do?" Al asked.

Bud answered, "Florida has an open-range law. Makes the driver responsible for all livestock. You hit 'em, you pay." This technical report on the state of Florida's regulations quieted everyone. Finally, Paul reassumed his leadership role.

"Well, that animal is dead and we can't change that. Standing here in the rain isn't the answer either. She's not a traffic hazard there in the ditch, and the car is sitting here in the middle of the road."

Car owners captured in a casual, unposed snapshot at Cecil Field, Jacksonville, Florida, 1947, while planning a trip to the beach. Left to right: Duty Driver, Bud Rich, Al Fox, D. K. Tooker, and Paul Hayek.

There was no dissent. The unintentional butchers climbed back into the car, soaked to the skin, and proceeded to Cecil Field. The car drove just fine, as any tank would after running into a smaller object. The incident was reported to the officer of the day, who made an official notation in his log. Later, a letter was written by the Navy Base Administration Section to the appropriate agency, but the incident died along with the unfortunate cow.

Night driving in heavy rain was voted by the group, particularly the duty driver, as "unsavory and to be avoided in the future."

With that lesson learned, the weekends continued to be the perfect relaxation medium for the carpooling beach commuters. The small select group attracted envious

Beach plans completed and all personnel aboard, the Blooper is pointed toward Jax Beach, bathing suits at the ready.

notice and was often the main attraction every Saturday morning in their bachelor quarters' parking lot. Just watching them prepare for a beach outing always brought out a fair-sized audience. Each pilot had a job assignment. Al Fox would fuel up at the base service station, checking all fluid levels. Bud Rich would purchase the beer and ice along with some snacks, with help from me, and then carefully load them into the two .50-caliber ammo boxes. The boxes were securely fastened to the Blooper's trunk rack at the rear of the car. Soft drinks were always included, both for the duty driver and for any of the girls who might feel that soft drinks were safer. It is important to note here that the libations were all in *bottles.*

Paul Hayek would tend to items that demanded planning and decision making. Other than that, his only actual hands-on duty was to insure that the bathing suits were tied tightly to the door handles so they would not fly off during the high speeds attained en route to Jax Beach. The lifeguards there were very stringent and enforced the wearing of suits, usually—but that's another story.

When the duty driver was ready, all car owners would pile in and issue the departing cry: "Away, driver, and don't spare the horses!" There being only sixty-five horses available, sparing them wasn't always an easy thing. Fortunately, Florida was as flat then as it is now.

July came and went, and August was rolling by too quickly for everyone concerned. What with the car as the main attraction, free refreshments, and dashing (their word again) fighter pilots, the need to cruise the beach sands in the girl round-up maneuver was no longer necessary. A spot just south of the pier was famous, by then, as the party center. Often, upon the ceremonious arrival of the creaking vehicle, girls would already have placed their beach towels provocatively near where the pilots would park their car.

Only one weekend was lost, because of another torrential rain due to a hurricane passing just off the coast. Since none of the guys wanted to risk another cow-killer mission, a "sacrifice" was made to the Rain God. Instead of fun in the sun, the pilots hosted a costume party at the "O" Club and invited several attractive lady guests. It was rated by all as highly successful.

The last weekend of that August in 1947 turned out to be especially memorable, in a summer rich in memories of the beach, the girls, and, of course, the Blue Blooper. After another happy day, all guests had been delivered home safely to their concerned mothers and the Blooper was making its resolute journey home in the competent hands of the duty driver (whose name, the careful reader will note, is not of record). Bud, Paul, and I were asleep in the back, as usual. Al had drawn the dreaded "brake person" duty, along with the assignment of keeping the driver awake. It was about 10:30 on that Sunday evening.

"Duty Driver," Al said, "it's really hot tonight." The driver nodded. A few minutes later Al continued: "It's too hot. Something's wrong. The floor boards are burning my feet."

Suddenly, the duty driver exclaimed, "I think we've got a fire here. I can see some flames through the floor!"

"Pull over!" Al yelled, cruelly waking up the passengers in the rear seats. As the Blooper slowed and was skillfully maneuvered to the side of the narrow road, it was obvious to even the most casual observer that there were flames in the engine compartment. The car was definitely on fire.

"Bail out!" the commanding voice of Paul ordered, and all hands did just that. Al grabbed Paul's bathing suit from the door handle to use as a pot holder and raised one side of the hood. The flames leaped higher with the sudden influx of more air.

"Do we have a fire extinguisher?" somebody shouted. Of course, there was none. The 1924 antique was in serious trouble and no one had a clue as to what to do next. Paul's flailing at the combustion with a beach towel had no effect except to destroy the towel.

It was cool-hand Bud who saved the day. Awakening from a sound sleep, he'd seen the flames shooting up from the front of the car. He made an instantaneous decision. To the amazement of his peers, Bud suddenly leapt up and out onto the front edge of the roof, holding one of the ammo boxes high above his head.

"Take cover," he yelled, and emptied the contents over the exposed side of the flaming engine. The remaining beer and soda pop bottles, along with the rest of the ice, now melted, plummeted down and exploded against the engine block. The fire was suddenly all but extinguished. A few little spurts of flame remained, these being some burning wiring. Bud took care of these with another dousing from the remaining ammo box.

A flashlight revealed a broken fuel line, which had allowed gasoline to stream against the very hot engine block. The car was saved, and Bud Rich was proclaimed "man of the hour," many times over.

The Blue Blooper was pushed (not an easy task) farther to the side of the road and left for the night. The very same Marine captain of the fine 1941 blue Chevy happened along just then and carried the inferno survivors to their quarters. He even agreed to tow the fire-ravaged vehicle next morning to the base, where the wiring and gasoline tubing were replaced. But for some reason the car never ran quite as well after the fire episode.

The pilots' operational training phase ended a few weeks later, and the vintage car owners were soon separated by official orders to their individual new duty stations. It was a sad moment as the pilots bade farewell to the Blue Blooper. Even the designated driver seemed to have something in his eye for a minute, when, offered for sale, it fell to other hands.

The new owners clearly did not understand or appreciate the rich potential of the Blue Blooper. They evidently thought that it was just a car. Later reports from Cecil Field failed to mention anything about any more exciting beach parties . . . just south of the pier.

10 Which Way Is Highway Fifty South?

R escuing a downed or injured pilot is always a challenge. Rescues far out at sea are the most difficult and usually unsuccessful. However, when the pilot is less than four miles from his departed airfield, the chances for a successful retrieval are pretty good. At least, you'd think so.

In 1958 Capt. John Hubner, USMC, took off from the Naval Air Station near Olathe, Kansas, leading a flight of three F9F-8T Panther jets. He was the instructor, and his two wingmen were transitioning from props to jets.

The briefing was thorough. As the flight became airborne, having raised their landing gear and flaps and climbing through three hundred feet, the leader pressed the microphone key:

"This is Charlie One. I've got smoke in the cockpit, and the TPT"—tailpipe temperature—"is pegged."

"Roger, Leader. You've also got fire coming out of the tailpipe," came from one of his wingmen.

"It's burning real good, Charlie One," this from the other wingman.

John's thoughts and actions were automatic; he had rehearsed for this very situation many times. "I've got to get to five hundred feet and eject; but if I wait too long, this thing will blow," he reasoned.

He reduced power, disconnected the various straps and radio cords, said a quick prayer, and pulled the face curtain. As he exited the aircraft, the seat separated automatically and the chute snapped open with a hard jolt. He oscillated only once before hitting the ground. He had landed in a recently plowed field. As he gathered in his parachute, he could see a huge black, mushrooming cloud rising not more than half a mile away, graphically showing where his Grumman aircraft had also met the ground.

A quick personal inventory revealed no apparent broken bones and only some facial scratches, which were bleeding slightly. As he wondered about what had just happened, he glanced around, noting that he had just missed hitting a barbed-wire fence by about ten feet and that a secondary dirt road was situated on the other side of the fence.

He carefully climbed over the fence strands and folded his nylon life-saving chute on the top of the barbed wire. He then took off his hard hat, placed it on a fence post, and sat down to wait for the rescue he knew was at hand.

In less than ten minutes, he first heard, then saw, the navy ambulance tearing down the dirt road toward him. The siren was screaming and the red lights were flashing brightly. As the driver approached the scene, he slammed on the brakes and cranked down the window.

"Which way is Highway 50, south?" the medic shouted.

John, not wishing to point out the obvious—his bleeding face, the parachute draped over the fence behind him, the helmet sitting sentinel-like on the fencepost—replied:

"It's about three quarters of a mile back down this road, bearing right at the intersection."

"Thanks," said the rescue man; with this emotional outpouring, he slammed the ambulance in reverse and negotiated a difficult 180-degree turn, then disappeared in a cloud of dust to the south, presumably headed for Highway 50.

John, after a few moments of serious pondering, figured that (a) the driver was not properly briefed; (b) the driver was not too bright; (c) he suffered from poor eyesight; or (d) all of the above. He decided on (d) as the most logical choice.

A farmer's house was not too far away, and after climbing back over the wire fence, he calmly walked to the house and telephoned the operations duty officer, who picked up John himself, in less than twenty minutes.

"How come the ambulance didn't pick you up?" the duty officer had asked.

"Apparently he had some more pressing business on Highway 50," was John's only comment.

Note: The ambulance driver must still be headed for Highway 50 South, because John never did learn why he had been a "second-choice rescuee."

11   A Motto to Die For?

"Excuse me, Major, the Colonel wants to see you right away, Sir. He says it's important."

"Thank you, Lieutenant. Tell him I'll be right there. I want to get out of this flight gear first." The latter had, as the old song goes, "The slight aroma of performing seals."

Our Marine fighter squadron, VMF-323, was operating out of NAS, Atsugi, Japan. It was July 1963, and the weather in the Tokyo-Yokohama area was sticky hot and so humid that a newly starched uniform would pretty much wilt in only an hour.

The SDO (Squadron Duty Officer) had informed me that my presence was required by the CO. I was the squadron executive officer and second in command. However, this meant little when Lt. Col. Claude Barnhill summoned. He expected prompt action from all of his subordinates, even from someone in such a lofty position as mine.

Five squadron pilots in flight gear with G suits and helmet bags. Left to right: 1st Lt. Phil Kruse, Capt. "Nabe" Allen, Maj. D. K. Tooker, Capt. Dick Ritchie, 1st Lt. Tom McClay.

We had trained as a unit for the previous year in the States for our present mission, that of becoming a precise, smoothly operating squadron, completely combat ready. We weren't exactly patterned after a prisoner-of-war camp, but then we were no Club Med either—perhaps somewhere in between. Each pilot had successfully completed a USN-mandated flying and ground school syllabus to best provide him with the tools to fly one of the fastest supersonic fighters in the world, the F8U-2NE Crusader (later designated the F8E). Morale was high and each pilot more than ready to give his 110 percent. We were an all-weather squadron, which was fortunate as the poor flying conditions in Japan were legendary. Each pilot was also carrier-qualified along with Sidewinder missile and 20-mm cannon

A flight of six F-8 Crusaders over Okinawa, 1963: the squadron's answer to the Blue Angels.

expertise. Many pilots wore a patch on their flight suits that stated: "F8U, the Last of the Gun Ships." The story behind this patch was that the F-4 Phantom jet fighter was about to be introduced into the navy's aircraft inventory. It was faster, about 2.0 mach compared to 1.6 mach, had a much better radar with almost three times the acquisition range, carried more missiles, and even had a back-seat man to operate the radar and make coffee. But a huge difference existed—it carried no guns. This deficiency was later corrected during the Vietnam War, when it was no longer acceptable. In the meantime, in friendly competition our pilots never let the F-4 pilots forget that if they needed cover from someone with "real" guns, we would be glad to come to their rescue with F-8 Crusaders.

But, as Max Schulman always wrote, "I digress." The colonel was still awaiting my presence. Having changed uniforms fairly successfully, that is, without a needed shower, I padded from the pilot's locker room over to the CO's office in another part of the hangar. I presented myself smartly to Lieutenant Colonel Barnhill.

"Good morning, Sir. You wanted to see me?"

"Yeah, sit down, D. K. I think we have a problem and I wanted your thoughts on it."

I quickly flipped through my mental files, using up only milliseconds to explore some of the possibilities. Our squadron flight surgeon had been thrown out of the officers' club the previous evening for carrying a large bowl of smoldering maple leaves into the dining room. He thought we needed to be reminded of the autumnal aromas of home. The senior navy staff duty officer didn't agree, unfortunately. The only other incident that came to mind was that of Acting Corporal Fitzgerald, who had gotten in trouble again in the "village" (a Marine word for "town") for being drunk, and the MPs had returned him to the base under arrest. This was the third or fourth time for Fitzgerald, hence the "acting." He'd had his stripes removed so many times he had a least four different shirts with different rates sewed on his sleeves. What made this otherwise simple disciplinary problem difficult was that Fitzgerald was one of the finest jet mechanics in the naval service. He could diagnose and troubleshoot a jet engine like no one else just by listening to it. It didn't hurt his credibility much, either, that he was one of the colonel's favorite guys. He was for sure a very likable Irishman.

"If it's about Fitzgerald, Sir, I can take care of it. I'll have a talk with him and see. . . ."

"No, D. K., that's not what I want to discuss with you. I'm sure you'll handle that matter just fine. I know he's a good man. Wish we had more like him. No, this is a bit more serious." A long pause, perhaps for effect.

"Our squadron doesn't have a motto." He let this sink in. "I've done some research and no one has been able to come up with one, at least one that's been officially assigned by the Navy Department. We've got our "Death Rattlers" insignia along with those yellow diamonds we paint on our aircraft. That all looks great! Best insignia in the Marine Corps, maybe the whole navy." To voice disagreement here would have been not only disloyal but stupid.

"You're right, Colonel," I'm certain I sounded sincere. "But I don't believe every squadron has a motto."

"Of course they don't! That's not the point, but I think ours should have a motto. We can have a separate patch for the flight suits and leather flight jackets made up. Most of those Japanese tailor shops specialize in making patches. In fact, we could put it on our squadron blazers that the Doc is having made up at that shop just outside the gate . . . J. B. Tan, isn't it?"

"No, Colonel, it's James Lee." I paused for a moment, not wishing to sound contradictory. "It's right next door to J. B. Tan's, I believe."

"OK, whatever. I know they do excellent work."

There was a moment's pause while the colonel signed some papers that Captain Ritchie, the adjutant had tiptoed in with. I was hoping that when the colonel found out about the smoking maple leaves, he would remember the fine work the Doc (Lt. Alan Eberstein, USNR(MC)) was doing besides his flight surgeon duties. Coordinating the ordering of thirty-four squadron blazers, one for each officer in the unit, was no small achievement. Getting all thirty-four to agree on anything would be unique, inasmuch as each officer could choose his desired style of the sports jacket, single- or double-breasted, and even the buttons. The blazers were a vivid cobalt blue, recommended by Doc and cast in concrete by the CO's approval, that wouldn't match any article of clothing that side of the Pacific Ocean. However, the lining was the real startler. It was an eye-shattering explosive gold. It looked brighter than most state capitol roofs and had a reflective quality just short of a polished hallway mirror. On the credit side of this madness, it assured that each pilot and ground officer would wear the blazer *only* to authorized squadron functions. He wouldn't wear it to bed, to a street fight, or to any similar important function. But at squadron parties, whenever the designated party director yelled "Gold side out!" some thirty officers would stand up and turn their jackets inside out, the shining gold lining thus revealed. Women would faint while strong men gasped. Invariably at air force officers' clubs (if not the navy's) we always received a round of applause.

(Note: I still have my blazer and wear it about every ten years to VMF-323's squadron reunions, even though it's a little snug in places.)

But again, I digress. The adjutant departed and the colonel eyed me expectantly for an answer, one that hadn't even dimly seen the light of day.

He spoke: "I remember one from somewhere that was in Latin, something like, 'Death Before Dishonor,' and another one about 'Don't Let the Bastards Grind You Down.' But I've seen that one on every guy's desk doing paperwork in Washington."

"Yes, Sir," I nodded wisely, hoping for a little more direction. In the past few minutes my devious mind deduced that, first, we probably didn't really need a Latin catchphrase; and second, I was sure he was going to unload this motto mission on me, which I reasoned would put it (the mission) somewhere between fruitless and career-ending. But I wasn't about to tell the captain how to steer his ship. Suddenly, the light over my head came on.

"Colonel, I've got an idea. Why not let the pilots in on this? Let them participate. They'll come up with some suggestions. I'll check with Headquarters to make sure we're not copying some other outfit. If you and I decide arbitrarily, they might feel that we're forcing it down their throats."

I hoped he hadn't noticed that I'd placed myself cleverly in the "we" category, as in "you and me, Colonel."

"Excellent, D. K., good idea. I agree with you right down the line. The democratic way isn't the military way, but in this case I think it just might be the best plan."

"Colonel, one more thing. I feel that a little motivational talk from you would get the ball rolling—perhaps at our next AOM"—all officers meeting—"this afternoon. It's already scheduled. I'll tell Tony"—the operations officer—"to cancel the NAV lecture and I'll cut my remarks to the bare minimum."

I conducted those meetings and, on cue, the colonel would enter the ready room as we came to attention. He always had the last word, which left no doubt in anyone's mind who was running the show.

"Set it up, D. K., 1600 hours you said. I'll have something to say." My inner voice, the one that sometimes gets me in trouble, was also heard to say "Surprise, surprise," but fortunately my lips never moved.

The colonel gave his little all-officers talk, and he was inspirational, to say the least. No one was sobbing openly, but everyone was respectfully attentive. I couldn't read their reactions, and so at happy hour later that evening I approached my good friend, confidant, and designated squadron skeptic, Capt. T. R. Moore.

Lt. Col. Claude O. Barnhill, Commanding Officer, VMF-323, Atsugi, Japan, July 1963. No motto yet.

"What did you think, T. R., about the colonel's search for a good squadron motto?"

"It's bullshit, D. K." T. R. was not known for an inability to express opinions. "Why the hell do we need a motto? We're fighter pilots, our job is to kill other pilots in the air and bad guys on the ground. Besides, who knows Latin anymore?"

"Don't hold back, T. R. Tell me your innermost thoughts." I was actually a little angry with him, partly because I agreed with his assessment. "If you get any huffier, I'll assign *you* to run this little exercise."

"You wouldn't do that, would you, D. K.?"

"No, but I might ask you for some help. You're aware that my assignment wasn't exactly volunteer in nature?"

"Yeah, well, let's run this by the Doc. He'll have some ideas, I'm sure."

Great, I thought. Some bright thoughts from our always-in-trouble flight surgeon.

"Let's talk tomorrow, T. R. It's almost dinnertime now. We'll bring some food back for the Doc—he's restricted."

"I didn't know. Was that because of the burning leaves episode?"

"They were only smoldering, T. R. But, yes, the navy captain thought it prudent that the charismatic surgeon remain out of the club and dining room for a week. This was in lieu of an official letter. So, I agreed and the Doc agreed, but I haven't told Barnhill yet." With that, we went to dinner.

It would be convenient to be able to say that the dawn broke the following day clear and bright, with stunning suddenness. Actually, it sneaked up on us with a nasty moist little drizzle, which added to the already high humidity. But the "stunning suddenness" better sets the stage for the day's mission, that of deciding on an *appropriate* (the key word here) motto for a fighter squadron. I'd passed the word through T. R. that after dinner all the officers were to submit suggestions right away. I knew the skipper was anxious to resolve his ongoing dilemma of our mottolessness.

I missed breakfast that morning because of a necessary discussion with Acting Corporal Fitzgerald, thereby avoiding informal discussion of mottoes with my peers. He was properly recalcitrant and I was properly authoritative. "Corporal, this is your last chance (again)! Next time, and there better not be one, and you'll be a permanent private first class." He was so repentant that I felt a certain sympathy for him. On the other hand, I knew I'd be having this same conversation with him again, and I did.

Later in the day, in the squadron ready room, pilots were reading technical bulletins and NOTAMs, and several games of acey-deucey were in progress, along with briefings for the scheduled training flights. I interrupted their activities.

"OK, guys, as I told you, I need your ideas on an appropriate squadron motto by this evening. Pass them to T. R. or the Ops officer." I'd scheduled a short meeting with both officers in my quarters at 1800 hours. I knew I could count on my professionals to come through.

The Doc showed up at my room in the four-compartment divided Quonset hut forty-five minutes before the six o'clock meeting. He had a problem.

"D. K.," he began, "I'm pretty fed up, literally, with the chow at the PX and Ops slop chute." The latter was a loving name bestowed on the tiny snack bar in the airfield operations building. It would be charitable to say that it had a "limited" menu.

"Well, Doc, you made your own bed."

"I know, I know. But just bringing in some needed atmosphere to the "O" Club doesn't seem to warrant a week's restriction." I agreed with him, to a point.

"It was that or an official letter from the navy to Colonel Barnhill, which would have to go in your jacket. I thought I was doing you a favor, Doc." He nodded but obviously did not agree.

"Any chance you'll talk to the navy brass, maybe get my sentence commuted? You know, time off for good behavior?" The Doc couldn't always get along with the senior navy medical brass. He'd had more ups and downs with them than a Venetian blind.

"I'll look into it. Meantime, you got any brainstorms for a squadron motto?"

"Not really. Maybe 'Barney's Bastards' or perhaps 'Once a Knight, Always a Knight.'" We both knew the tag line: "Once a night is not enough." I thanked him and wished him a hearty *bon appétit* at the slop chute. The door closed behind him with just a hint of a frustrated shove.

T. R. and Tony Blair (the Ops officer) showed up on time. I poured them both a strong rum and coke with fresh lime. Both officers had excellent records, and Tony had just recently been selected for the rank of major. I felt I could count on both men. T. R. spoke first.

"D. K., we've scraped the barrel and beat the bushes for the best sources of motto suggestions." A pregnant pause. "I'm afraid the pickings were poor."

"How many responses did you actually get, T. R.?"

"Well, several." That told me a lot. "Actually, the lieutenants apparently got together and reached a unanimous selection."

"That's great, T. R. I was hoping we'd have some agreement. Makes my job a lot easier. You agree, Tony, with the selection?"

Tony avoided my question and stared at T. R. as if encouraging him to continue.

"Major, this wasn't my choice exactly, but I guess it's as good as any." I knew when he addressed me by my rank we had a problem. T. R. handed me a folded piece of paper, much as a jury foreman delivers a guilty verdict to the judge. I opened the paper with great care. It read: NEATNESS COUNTS.

Both men shuffled nervously, and both suddenly found extreme interest in the floating ice cubes in their drinks.

"Barnhill will kill me if I show him this. Are you sure this 'motto' was the consensus? Are the lieutenants trying to have their beloved executive officer shot?"

T. R. took a long pull at his beverage. Tony still had more ice cube research to perform.

"D. K., I swear that's what the guys came up with. I realize it does not sound very much like a fighting outfit's motto."

"You got that right, T. R." Tony, having solved the problem in his glass, finally spoke up.

"D. K., the way I read it, the guys don't feel a motto is all that necessary. They feel it's a bit pretentious, maybe too dramatic." 'Death Before Dishonor' doesn't do it either. We're sittin' in these cockpits trying to kill the other bastard before he kills us and trying to save our own ass at the same time. Honor was for the Boy Scouts, survival is for now. . . ."

I thought about the words that a suddenly eloquent Ops officer had spoken. I could not fault his logic nor his comments.

"You agree, T. R.?"

"Yes, Sir." He looked me straight in the eye.

"OK, which one of you wants to carry this message to Garcia?" The reaction here was "flinch." There were no takers, and our 1800 hours meeting was over.

I put off the inevitable, as any cowardly courier would do. If there was ever a case of "shoot-the-messenger" logic, this was it. I avoided the colonel basically most of the next two days. I flew extra hops, inspected the troops' barracks (twice), and attended the enlisted men's mess at noon. I even spent some time trying to contact the navy captain of the air station, to make some points on Doc's behalf. He was in nearby Yokosuka, where I wished I was.

Finally, the colonel cornered me on my way out of the hangar.

"D. K., how's that project going that we talked about the other day?" He started to get into his jeep.

"Well, Colonel, OK, I guess." I was stumbling already.

"The officers did come up with some ideas but nothing too splendid." Poor choice of words, I thought. "We might want to take a little longer, Sir."

"Nonsense. What have you got? You said you'd try to get a consensus, didn't you? Let's take a look." He knew I had something; he just didn't know what.

I handed him the ticking time bomb, T. R.'s note. His expression didn't change. He turned the yellow paper over several times as if there were more to read. Sadly, there wasn't. I read his lips as he climbed into his jeep, "Neatness counts?"

"I'll get back to you on this later, Major," and he drove off toward the officers' quarters. He never called me by my rank, it was always "D. K." or "Don." For sure, I've had it, I thought.

But I was wrong. The colonel never mentioned the subject of a squadron motto again, nor did he address me by rank again either. Perhaps, when he thought it over, he felt as the pilots did. We really didn't need a motto to wear on our flight suits. It was what was *inside* each pilot that counted, which sure as hell wasn't neatness.

EPILOGUE

Lt. Col. Claude O. Barnhill did not live to see any motto on our flight suits. He was killed in a jeep accident in the Philippines some nine months after this incident, in April of 1964.

For roughly the next twenty years, VMF-323 fighter squadron continued to serve without an official motto. Then, in the 1980s, they did adopt a patch that each squadron pilot wears today. It says simply, "Come to Fight, Come to Win." The colonel would have approved.

12 The Field Is Closed— What Are Your Intentions?

Every military pilot practices in-flight emergencies so that when they occur, and they will, it will be routine— old hat. Of course, they never are. But at least the pilot has thought about it, perhaps even gone through the procedures in his MOFT (Mobile Operational Flight Trainer). For example, there is a standard approved procedure to follow when the pilot sees his fire warning light suddenly come on. After the widely accepted "Oh, shit," he checks his engine instruments for excessive temperatures, looks in the mirror for telltale smoke or fire indications, then checks with his wingman (if he has one) and in twin engine aircraft (almost universal now) shuts down the offending engine. Needless to say, he heads for the nearest landing place at the earliest convenient moment.

But what about those circumstances that cannot be anticipated or trained for in advance? This is a story of just such

A flight of Crusaders en route to Atsugi, Japan. Bad weather lies ahead.

an incident. It owes its vividness of detail, despite the passage of almost forty years, to the fact that it happened to me and my wingman.

Marine Fighter Squadron 323 had been deployed overseas as a "combat ready" unit. After a year's locked-on intensive training in the United States, the squadron had arrived at their home base in Atsugi, Japan, in June 1963. Their mission was to be instantly deployable to any trouble spot in the Far East. From the airfield near the Yokohama-Yokosuka Complex, their eighteen aircraft were assigned as strip alert (five minutes maximum to become airborne) carrier deployments, operations in Okinawa, Taiwan, and the Philippines. The twenty-eight pilots kept their bags packed. The aircraft assigned to this combat ready unit was the supersonic, single-seat F8E. It carried four air-to-air Sidewinder missiles and four 20-mm cannons. To say that the pilots were pleased with their Chance Vought–built Crusaders would be an understatement.

On one day in September 1963, the squadron had just completed two weeks of round-the-clock GCI (ground controlled intercept) radar training on the island of Okinawa some nine hundred miles south of their home base in Japan. Sixteen of the eighteen Crusaders were in commission, with two aircraft down for routine maintenance. The "lucky" sixteen pilots donned their flight gear and prepared for the forthcoming briefing. Those unlucky enough not to be scheduled to fly had to fly home in the KC-130 transports with the ground support personnel. There were always more pilots than planes, as is the custom in U.S. Navy and Marine flight units.

The squadron flight surgeon, Lt. Alan Eberstein (with a *B*), USN, had already left the airfield at Naha, Okinawa, for Atsugi in the first of two KC-130s. He was to play an important role later in this story.

"Tony, what's the Atsugi weather?" the commanding officer, Claude O. Barnhill, had asked his operations officer.

"I just checked with aerology, Skipper. The last weather sequence reported fifteen thousand feet overcast, seventy-five hundred feet scattered, with fifteen miles visibility," Captain Blair had replied.

"Sounds pretty good. I think we'll put on a flyover for our less fortunate navy friends at the air station. What do you guys think?"

The assembled pilots nodded in agreement. No one was stupid enough to suggest that a flyover might require some rehearsing or that it was a lot of extra effort, or that some of the guys might be a bit strung out from the two weeks of intense, all-out flying.

"Right on, Skipper," was the overwhelming consensus. A democratically run fighter squadron is like that.

Aircraft assignments were made, the short briefing completed, and all sixteen pilots checked off their names under the "out" column on the flight board. The hop—scheduled flight time one hour, forty-five minutes—across the East China Sea and Pacific Ocean was under way. The time was 3:10 P.M.

The first flight of four F-8 Crusaders was led by the colonel, as always. First to fly, first to fight, and first to land. Captain Tony Blair, of operations fame, was in charge of the second division of four, and Captain T. R. Moore headed group three. The final four "intrepids" were pleased, no doubt, to have me as their leader.

Our briefing was to fly each individual division (of four aircraft) to a rendezvous point some thirty-five miles southeast of our home base. This point, a navigational aid, was called Fukuoka Control. Probably a lovely place in the spring, we would of course see it in the fall. We were to circle there, left-hand orbit at our cruising altitude of flight level 360 (36,000 feet).

The first twelve fighters got off the ground in good order, joined up, and headed for the rendezvous. My wingman and squadron adjutant, Capt. Dick Ritchie, had a starting problem with his aircraft and our flight was delayed about ten minutes. Not to worry, I thought; I knew a shortcut (just kidding).

Soon after becoming airborne, I could hear the colonel talking to the other flight leaders. Everyone was in a "we-won't-be-late-for-happy-hour" frame of mind, although my flight was a little late. We were in the catching-up mode and had a little more throttle laid on.

"Checker One from Black Ace One, what's your TACAN"—a UHF navigation system—"reading on Fuka Control, over?" The colonel wanted to know if I knew where I was. I did.

"Roger, Black Ace, am reading 120 miles on the two-forty-degree radial of Fukuoka TACAN."

"OK, Checker. I'm about fifteen minutes out from the navigational fix, Fuka-whatever. We'll orbit left as briefed. I'm still at flight level three six zero. Over."

"Rog, Skipper. Break, Break, have you checked the weather yet? Looks like some heavy stuff out to the west, maybe thunder bumpers, over."

"Yeah, Checker One. I've been watching, too. I'm switching to Atsugi Approach Control again for a weather check. Tried earlier but too far away, I guess."

The radios were all quiet as the colonel attempted to get an up-to-date weather report. It had been more than three hours since the last Atsugi weather synopsis. The reason he and I were yakking and not the other flight leaders was because as second senior pilot, I would have to take over the entire flight of sixteen for the planned flyover, should the CO's radio conk out.

Several minutes later Barnhill's voice filled our helmets: "Checker One and Flight: Atsugi reports fifteen thousand broken, three thousand overcast, one and a half mile's vis and light rain." I had no answer for this downturn of events, but I transmitted anyhow.

"Roger, Black Ace Leader. I copy weather. Sounds like their aerology department went to sleep." I didn't know what else to say. Evidently a fast-moving cold front had decided to visit our air station. None of the other fourteen pilots had anything to say either, as they let their commanding officer and the executive officer hash things over. We were rapidly approaching the airfield's minimum instrument landing conditions at the *single* runway known as Atsugi Naval Air Station, our home away from home.

"Black Ace from Checker One. Well, that simplifies things, I guess. We can do that flyover on a better day. Are you still at three six zero?"

"Affirmative, Checker. I've got all twelve in sight here, holding at flight level three six zero. As soon as you've got us in sight, call me."

A few moments of silence while the boss man did some mental planning. It wasn't the end of the world, and we still had sufficient fuel to make the mandatory instrument let-downs to the final GCA (ground controlled approach) landing. A major consideration was obvious, though. You just didn't show up suddenly with sixteen aircraft in bad weather over the approach fix, which until a few moments ago didn't know it was bad weather. Another item of interest: Aerology reported that the weather had deteriorated all over. There would be no alternate airfield to land at. We were committed to the Atsugi runway.

"This is Black Ace Leader to Flight: We'll switch to Control"—he never could pronounce Fukuoka—"and make our instrument approaches by section (two aircraft). The lowest fuel-state aircraft will go first. Checker Flight, you'll be last since your group took off last."

I affirmed his message and listened as each pilot radioed his exact fuel state in pounds to Black Ace. My three wingmen signaled visually to me how their remaining fuel stood. In general we had about thirty to thirty-five minutes remaining—at altitude. Once we started downhill on the landing approach, the jet engine would become less efficient, burning fuel at a much faster rate.

Two by two, the jet fighters departed from the 36,000-foot holding pattern to lower altitudes as directed by Approach Control. They must have been taken aback by the sudden arrival of sixteen aircraft, but the Japanese controllers' voices did not reveal any noticeable concern, only their usual problem of pronouncing words with the letter *L* in them.

Twenty minutes went by before our flight was cleared to begin our approach. Capt. Dick Wahl, my Number Three Man, and his wingman, Capt. Wendy Grubbs, had lower fuel states than Captain Ritchie and I did, so they went first. I thought, "Well, better last than never." It was almost 5:30 now and I knew it would be dark soon on the ground—where I wished I was.

Ritchie reported visually that he was down to a thousand pounds of fuel, with the low-fuel warning light on. We called it the "panic button." Mine had already been on for several minutes.

We pushed over, reduced power to 80 percent, extended the speed brakes, and started down the hill, the final twenty thousand feet. I figured it would take about five hundred pounds for the approach, with enough left to taxi in without flaming out, always a very embarrassing moment.

The weather was really terrible, not so turbulent but with heavy, heavy rain. My wingman practically had his left wingtip in my cockpit. He wasn't going to lose me, no matter what. We had already briefed, as was standard operating procedure, for the wingman to take a landing interval as soon as he could see the runway. The Atsugi runway was too narrow to land in section, that is, in formation.

"This is your final GCA Controller, Checker One and Two. Do not acknowledge any further transmissions. You are on glide path, three and one-half miles from touchdown on Runway Zero One. Weather is one-half mile visibility with rain. Advise poor braking action. You are coming left of center line, your new heading zero one five. You are slightly below glide slope, bring it up, please. You are now on centerline and glide path."

Suddenly in the background I heard someone else yell, "Checker Four just took the Morest gear. Runway closed! Runway closed!" This was immediately followed by:

"This is your GCA Controller. Wave off, wave off! Plane in front of you has engaged the arresting gear. Runway fouled."

I added power just as we broke out from under the clouds and we flew down the single but obstructed runway. A Crusader was sitting smack in the middle of the runway with the heavy link chain stretched out behind it forming an inverted V. "We're screwed," I told my oxygen mask and then remembered I had a wingman. I'd been locked on to flight instruments so intently I hadn't so much as glanced his way. His visor was down so I couldn't see his eyes—probably a good thing. My fuel quantity gauge said, "Landing would be good here!" Translated, the four hundred pounds meant about four to six minutes left before having to eject.

"Checker One, I say again, the field is closed. What are your intentions?"

"Stand by, GCA," was all I could muster for the moment. I signaled Ritchie for his fuel state. He held up five fingers (for five hundred pounds), and I nodded. My needle was on the low side of four hundred, and at sea level the jet engine was gobbling up the JP-5 fuel rapidly.

"Switching to guard channel, Checker Two." No time to bid a fond farewell to the GCA guy. He was now out of the loop. Mentally I'd gone over this scenario previously, and now that my Number Four man, Wendy Grubbs, had taken the "gear" that closed the field, our two birds were in trouble. I'd kick his ass later. The Yokota Air Force Base was located directly ahead about sixteen nautical miles, with nice long runways, and was normally available for situations just like this. Unfortunately, the NOTAMs had announced that the airfield was closed "due to heavy equipment on runways while undergoing resurfacing."

"Hang in there, Dick." He'd just shown me four fingers. I chose not to show him my three. "We'll try Yokota; if no luck, we'll head out to sea on a one six zero degrees heading, put it on autopilot, and eject."

He nodded but I detected a certain reticence in his nod.

"Yokota Tower, Checker One, flight of two F-8s about four minutes south, fifty feet. Atsugi closed, low fuel state. Over." I only hoped someone was on duty in the tower.

"Roger, Checker One, your position. Advise the field is closed. Trucks on all main runways. Over." At least *they* didn't ask me my intentions.

"Roger, understand. Are the taxiways clear? Over." A moment's silence while the tower operator thought this one over.

"Well, that's affirm, but our crash equipment is not available, and . . ." I cut him short.

"OK, Dick, when we cross their field boundary, I'm going to make a 90- 270-degree turn. That should put us just over the parallel taxiway next to Runway 19. Take your interval as I line up on final. If it quits, just pull up and punch out." A double click told me he understood my transmission.

The ground flitted by below with occasional snapshots of green and soggy brown as we crossed the Yokota airfield's perimeter road. A 90-degree turn to the right for thirty seconds and then a nice, coordinated turn back left for 270 more hair-raising degrees toward what I hoped would be the beginning of a taxiway. I was half on instruments and half flying visually, usually a deadly combination.

Bingo! Runway 19, complete with a big cement truck right at the numbers. A quick bank to the right, level the wings, land long—'cause my faithful wingman was right on my ass. Almost ten thousand feet later I calmly turned off the very narrow taxiway (about forty-five feet wide; runways are usually two hundred feet wide) onto the concrete tarmac and taxied smartly up to airfield operations, where nobody was there to greet two very relieved Marine pilots. As we climbed down from the cockpits, I looked over at Dick. He wasn't smiling. He'd held up three fingers signifying about three to four minutes before flame-out. I'd ended up with two hundred pounds remaining—all of this was assuming the gauges to be accurate. I wondered in a sick way whether Captain Ritchie would have considered a flyby for the local air force personnel before our routine taxiway landing.

A nervous tower operator and a relieved operations duty officer let us use their telephone. I called squadron and Captain Blair answered.

"I figured you'd ejected. We listened to you on our base radio. Where'd you land? I know the runways were closed and . . ."

The "getaway" car—a fast 1953 Chevy—at Atsugi, Japan, 1963. Excellent transportation when properly operated. Seen here in winter hibernation.

"Tony, we're at Yokota, come and get us." (He shared a vintage automobile with the Doc, a 50-50 ownership.) "I'll explain all later. Bring a libation plus two pair of clean shorts." He ignored this. "And kick Wendy's ass, or I will when we get back."

"That's a big affirm, Checker. The Marines are on the way. I'll let you deal with Wendy. Did you remember to close out your flight plan?"

"Goddamnit, Tony. You think this is my first ever taxiway landing? It was routine, run of the mill, and it will become part of our squadron training syllabus. Don't forget the booze," and I hung up. The air force duty officer looked at me but wisely didn't say a word.

Fifty-five minutes later, a fast late-model 1953 black Chevy braked to a stop in front of the airfield operations building. Dick and I bade a brisk farewell to the air force types who were guarding their "closed" field and piled into the warmth and cheer of the Chevrolet's back seat. Dick, who didn't drink, took the first bite of some Old Grand-Dad or whatever it was. I, being a senior officer and aware of decorum and such, didn't bother to wipe the neck of the bottle before taking my turn. As the car lurched forward, I noticed that Tony might possibly have checked the whiskey supply as to its proper age and proof. And oh, guess who was riding copilot? Why yes, it was the famous squadron doctor, Flight Surgeon Eberstein, with a *B*, as he always said. In fact, it was *his* medicinal Old Grand-Dad that we were gratefully partaking of.

The Doc was highly thought of by the entire squadron, officers and men alike. His occasional craziness helped him relate to us pilots. He had a sign on his door at our Quonset hut that read: "Friendly ol' Doc Eberstein: Specializing in sex change operations, circumcisions repaired, midwife duties (Wednesdays only)." Versatile, was Doc. The right medicine every time.

It was quiet in the getaway car for a moment as Tony maneuvered his way out through the air force main gate without hitting either of the two sentries. A left turn and we were headed down the narrow, poorly designed Japanese road to our mutual home, Atsugi Base, with its renowned single runway. A steady rain was coming down and it was legally dark out.

Tony spoke first. "Well, you guys look a little limp. How much fuel did you land with finally?" Dick and I looked at each other uncertain as to our response. I volunteered. "I guess we had about thirty minutes left, maybe forty. How about you, Dick?" He wiped his mouth, devilishly feeling his drink, and said:

"About the same, I guess. Maybe a little more." The Doc looked back at us from the front seat with his peculiarly alert but skeptical gaze. Diagnosis: Liars? Smashed already? A little of both, perhaps.

"Tony, how long did it take them to clear the arresting gear and reopen the field?" I asked.

"About fifteen minutes, I think." My not too nimble brain processed this information. It was easy. The airfield would have opened for business some ten minutes or so *after* Dick and I would have ejected. I changed the subject.

"The Skipper pissed?" I asked.

"No," Tony said. "He headed for the club right after he landed. He either didn't know Wendy took the gear or else figured you guys would get down OK."

I decided that the CO had complete trust in my aeronautical leadership skills and then managed to wrench what was left of the Old Grand-Dad bottle from the nondrinking Captain Ritchie.

Since this was just another day at the mill, the conversation turned to more important things. Tony was complaining.

"The goddamned windshield wiper sticks! The wind keeps it stuck to the left," he was saying as he periodically poked his head out of his side window, trying to see into the driving rain. Visibility was no better here than on final approach at Atsugi. Only we could, if we wanted, pull over and stop. Obviously no fighter pilot would consider this indignity even a possible course of action. Home base was calling.

Tony's highway navigation problem was fast becoming a

serious dilemma, and the Doc, quiet up till then, proclaimed the obvious solution: "We need a manually operated windshield wiper." It was apparent to all that the resident doctor had taken *his* turn at the quart of spirits, too.

"Hold a steady course, Tony. I'll be right back." So saying, he climbed out of the opened copilot's window and somehow straddled the car roof, spread-eagled on his stomach. We watched in fascination as he moved the windshield wiper forth and back, and forth again, with one hand.

"Great, Doc, good work. I can see now. We're still on the road."

Tony was correct, but I was worried about the Doc sliding off the slippery wet, metal Chevy roof. I couldn't imagine how in the devil he was hanging on. Tony was driving slowly, maybe twenty-five to thirty miles an hour, but even at that speed a fall could take the crease out of the Doc's trousers.

Dick sat up and looked at me, his eyes at half-glaze.

"Where's Al, he asked?"

"Up on the roof," Tony replied. Dick belched and said something that sounded like "Oh."

About twenty minutes passed. Maybe it was an hour, who knows? The Doc must have been freezing, but if he was, he never let on. The only critical moment of our homeward journey came when the Doc demanded that refreshments be handed up to him. I watched in some fascination as Tony passed the bottle out his window and up to the Doc, who presumably took a swig and passed it back. Somehow, and this is the God's truth, the wiper never missed a beat. Just

Doc Eberstein (with a *B*) and Tony Blair strike a pose in the Blue Room to prepare for serious music appreciation. *Blair collection*

another routine ride home after a hard day's work.

We arrived at the Atsugi main gate where the Marine guards motioned us through without hesitation. Obviously they were used to seeing human windshield wiper personnel, in the rain, on top of 1953 Chevys.

Ten minutes later we were all sitting in the showers, fully clothed. The crease had vanished from the Doc's trousers. Tony's windbreaker was a dripping mess and my flight suit had somehow lost some of its luster. Dick was out like a light, propped up in the corner of the shower area with an odd smile on his face.

In the years that followed, I was never able to resolve which ride home was the most notable: the plane ride that took us to within moments of an ejection, or the automobile ride in the rain with the two crazies at the helm.

Epilogue

The career-saving taxiway landings at the kindly Yokota Air Force Base fortunately were not required again during our overseas tour. More remarkably, most of us completed Marine Corps careers and retired successfully, except Lt. Col. Barnhill, who died in a jeep accident several months later, and "Doc" Eberstein, who was killed in a Dallas car wreck in 1984. Lt. Col. Dick Ritchie died of a heart attack in 1991, and Tony Blair passed away in San Diego in June 2001. Me, I plan on living forever. So far, so good.

13 Runways Are Not Always One Way

Aircraft carriers as old as the CVA-16 of World War II fame often need to pull into a shipyard facility for repairs. Such was the case for the USS *Lexington* in April 1962. Sasebo, Japan, was the nearest port with a dry dock big enough to handle a ship of this size.

Since flight operations are a tad difficult during this in-port phase, the Carrier Air Group 14 commander, always referred to warmly as CAG, usually would off-fly some (or all) of his aircraft for repairs, modifications, or just general updating, as dictated by higher authority. Such was the case for eight fighter aircraft attached to VMF-323.

The marine squadron was just completing a six-month WESTPAC tour in the Far East. The F-8 Crusaders required, "at first availability," some work on their wing-folding mechanisms. This came under the heading of routine maintenance but had to be accomplished at a certified overhaul facility. Such was available at an enterprise called "Nippy Par," located at NAS Atsugi, Japan, near the Tokyo-Yokohama complex. (The name may have begun as Nippon Progressive Aircraft Rework, but it was Nippy Par to us.) The flight to Atsugi from the *Lex Maru* (the pilots' nickname) was uneventful—if carrier catapults, join-ups, bad weather, and landing at a strange field can ever be called "uneventful."

While their aircraft were being overhauled, the eight pilots waited. The waiting period stretched into seven days while they busied themselves with studying their aircraft operating manuals, listening to technical maintenance lectures, and occasionally venturing into the always comfortable Officers Club and bar. It was here that the various attributes of sister squadrons were debated. Somehow, "other" pilots never quite possessed the skills so expertly demonstrated by "our guys."

But it was finally over and, on a typical Japanese rainy morning in April, the pilots assembled for their briefing before returning to their overhauled carrier off the coast near Sasebo, some four hundred miles southwest. Just before they began manning aircraft, the CAG dispatched the Atsugi group to hold; there was bad weather in the aircraft recovery area.

The delay brought out the acey-deucey boards to help ease the five or six hours of hurry-up-and-wait. Along about 1400 hours (2:00 P.M.) it was decided by the CAG to have the eight Crusaders launch but to land at MCAS Iwakuni (near Hiroshima) and refuel there. It was 350 miles closer to where the carrier would be and perhaps in some better weather.

The two divisions of four each would be led by Lt. Col. Fred Watts, the commanding officer. On his wing was 1st Lt. Ed Dunn, and leading the second section of two was Capt. John Hubner, the squadron's LSO (landing signal officer), with 1st Lt. Al Shiner assigned to his wing.

Capt. T. R. Moore, USMC, stands beside his
F-8 Crusader on strip alert, NAS Atsugi,
1962. Note the live Sidewinder.
Moore collection

Capt. T. R. Moore headed the second division with three
more first lieutenants, Bobby Warren, Cliff Judkins, and
Zeke Baumgardner, on his wing. All of the pilots were proficient in bad weather flying, which they insisted was Japan's
only exported commodity. The two flights of four would
space their takeoffs thirty minutes apart so as not to overtax
the Approach Control and GCA (Ground Control Approach)
facilities at Iwakuni.

Friends from other squadrons came to see them off, as the
Lexington was scheduled to return to the States in a few short
weeks. The weather was forecast to be a thousand to fifteen
hundred feet overcast, three-quarters of a mile visibility in

light rain. Not exactly a piece of cake, but nothing the Marine pilots couldn't handle.

Upon their arrival at Iwakuni approach fix, Capt. T. R. Moore, with the second flight of four, checked in as briefed and was told to orbit at twenty thousand feet in a holding pattern. They were above the weather in the bright sunlight, wondering what was taking so long below. The half-hour separation should have been more than enough to land the first division of four Crusaders, since each approach would be made "in section" (two aircraft at a time), the wingman landing in formation with the section leader or taking a short interval on final. Apparently this wasn't happening.

The weather, when T. R. checked in by radio, was still reported as a thousand feet overcast with three-quarters of a mile visibility, in light-to-heavy rain. However, the actual weather conditions were more like two hundred feet overcast, one-quarter of a mile visibility.

"See you at the Club," T. R. radioed his flight. "We'll be making individual TACAN approaches, guys." The tactical air navigation instrument presented relative bearing and distance to the ground transmitter located right on the airfield. "Should be pretty poor braking condition, though, so stay alert."

As Approach Control had suggested making individual approaches, T. R. waved goodbye to his three wingmen. He pushed over, reduced power to 80 percent, and extended his speed brakes, still wondering what was going on below. He was assigned a different radio frequency and thus could not know that the weather was uncooperative at the airfield.

His final GCA Controller was still reporting a one-thousand-foot ceiling and a half-mile visibility as T. R. leveled off at the mandatory minimum altitude of two hundred feet.

Nothing but "muck and scud" (his words) as he added power for a go-around. About halfway down the runway, the clouds opened up a little and he could see the runway just below. For a moment he considered a 90- 270-degree maneuver whereby he would execute a starboard 90-degree turn for approximately thirty seconds, followed by a precision 270-degree turn to the port. Ideally, this would put him over the runway numbers but at the other end, for a landing in the opposite direction. This is a dicey, at best, solution but is sometimes a last resort maneuver. He made an instant decision vetoing this plan and climbed back up to the assigned twenty-thousand-foot holding pattern, prepared to try another approach. He'd have enough fuel for perhaps two more approaches.

His wingman, Lt. Bobby Warren, following behind him by several minutes, was now approaching the two-hundred-foot minimum altitude—except that he had not been passed off to a GCA controller. He was continuing a TACAN approach as he spotted a couple of breaks in the scudlike rain clouds below. The numbers (36) flashed by beneath him as he prepared to touch down on the end of the runway. He looked ahead into a foggy expanse, but as he was breathing the traditional sigh of relief in his oxygen mask, he suddenly spotted another F-8 rolling out toward him from the opposite direction. It was Lieutenant Shiner, the Number Four man in the first division. After a third attempt to land, he'd elected to execute the 90- 270-degree maneuver and had in fact been successful in finding the *other* end of the duty runway. Since the two aircraft were on different radio frequencies, neither knew of the other's presence.

Lieutenant Warren, without hesitation, jammed the throttle forward, causing the Crusader to leap skyward, with

The Iwakuni crash crew, ready for action, barrels down the duty runway, hot after Lieutenant Shiner in WS-202. *U.S. Navy photo*

just enough clearance to miss the other fighter. He then chopped power, not wanting to go around and chance another approach in the mung above, and concentrated on slowing down on the remaining length of the now two-way runway. Before he could breathe any further sighs of relief, a second problem loomed up, coming toward him in the very middle of the runway. It was a navy MB-1 crash truck, the largest made, obviously chasing after the Crusader that had just landed in the "wrong" direction.

Only Warren's afterburner saved a fiery collision on the runway. The F-8 staggered back in the air, and he could actually see the crash truck's occupants ducking as he roared overhead.

"Isn't anyone talking down here?" he yelled into his mask, but no one responded.

He then lowered the wing, raised his landing gear and flaps, and climbed up and away from the obvious confusion on the ground. At twenty thousand feet he re-entered the holding pattern and wondered what was next. His fuel was dangerously low, and he knew there was no alternate landing field available. He wondered why the crash truck had decided to play its version of "chicken" on the duty runway. Then he remembered the bay at the approach end of the runway and that other Crusader, traveling at a pretty good clip beneath him toward the water: hence, the ambulance-chasing actions of the crash vehicle. Slippery wet runways make for difficult braking, as all pilots know.

Lieutenant Shiner, as it happened, was not able to stop in time and dribbled off the end of the runway into a shallow five or six feet of seawater. The damage to the aircraft was minimal, and Shiner climbed out of the cockpit and crawled gingerly along the top of the fuselage and onto firm ground, where he was greeted by a dazed and somewhat shaken crash crew. Shiner's flight boots never got wet.

The score at halftime: One F-8 in the water (albeit, just barely), three on the ground, safely. The CO and his two wingmen had managed to make their GCA approaches just before the weather had deteriorated. Two aircraft with Lieutenants Judkins and Baumgardner ahead had remained in the initial holding pattern at twenty thousand feet after learning of the problems going on below. They had barely enough fuel to return to the Atsugi Airfield if they so chose. They did. That left Captain Moore and his wingman, Lieutenant Warren, still milling around between cloud layers at twenty thousand feet, deciding what their options might be as their fuel diminished by the minute.

The actual weather was so much worse than reported that the commanding officer, Lieutenant Colonel Watts, upon landing, had the GCA unit on the telephone. When the

Off the end and into the tidal basin: Lieutenant Shiner's WS-202, victim of bad weather and poor braking action, MCAS Iwakuni, Japan, 1962. *U.S. Navy photo*

"announced" weather was repeated, the colonel's response was an angry "You idiot! Open the door and *look* outside!" There was no reported response from the CGA officer to justify the "Alice in Wonderland" weather report.

Captain Moore called his wingman and suggested that they rendezvous between cloud layers, at what he remembered to be around twenty thousand feet. This would give them a chance to sort things out, hoping that perhaps the

Crash crew members who remembered to duck examine the damage to WS-202 (fortunately minimal). *U.S. Navy photo*

weather might break open long enough for the two of them to squeeze in. Moore estimated they had no more than twenty minutes of fuel remaining, and that meant that they were more or less committed to attempt additional instrument approaches. He learned that the other two Crusaders in his flight had departed for Atsugi. He was glad they'd decided to stay up high (burning much less fuel).

A check with Approach Control now revealed the true weather picture: horrible to worse, forward visibility limited to *less* than a quarter mile in fog. Had the pilots known this earlier, they would not have shot the approaches and would merely have returned to Atsugi, with plenty of fuel. Determining who screwed up on the ground would have to come later.

As the two pilots orbited the Iwakuni field in between two solid layers of clouds, the seriousness of their situation became evident. They would both have to eject in about fifteen minutes if the airfield remained closed because of the weather. Warren broke the tension:

"T. R., we've got company; your three o'clock, level. Looks like a KC-130 Tanker."

"Affirm, Bobby, got him in sight. Switch to Guard Channel. . . . break . . . break, Iwakuni Approach Control, we're switching to 243.0, out. . . . KC-130 Tanker vicinity of Iwakuni, this is Fireguard Five at twenty thousand feet, request your call sign. Over." A few seconds pause, and:

"Roger, Fireguard Five, this is Motherlode One Six. Over."

"Motherlode, Fireguard Five, we're a flight of two F-8s unable to land at Iwakuni due to weather. Request plug-ins. We're level at your nine o'clock. Over."

"Sorry, Fireguard, Wing SOP won't allow refueling when we're carrying passengers." Amazement silenced the two fighters, but only for a moment.

"Motherlode Tanker, we're Mayday! Roll out those baskets, *now*!"

A pause . . . then, "OK, Fireguard Flight. They're coming out. We'll maintain twenty grand and go to max power. Should give you two-forty, two-fifty knots. Over."

The two fighters quickly took their respective positions behind each of the two refueling baskets and plugged in. After receiving four thousand pounds of JP-5 fuel, they unplugged, with Warren tucked in tightly on Moore's wing as they climbed back up to an on-top altitude—just in time to see the setting sun disappear. They never found out what the Marine KC-130 Tanker was doing there or where it had been heading. The propitious aerial gas station was a sheer stroke of luck, cheating the ever lurking evil-weather gods out of their anticipated prey.

After refueling, Moore had pulled up abeam of the KC-130's cockpit and saluted the pilot with a quick but sincere arm movement. He was close enough to see the plane commander's "You're welcome" return salute. This saluting is not SOP or accepted flight procedure; however, it "seemed appropriate at the time," according to Captain Moore.

The return flight to Atsugi, their original departure point, was uneventful, if somewhat thoughtful in mood. The departed Point Oshima, the approach fix, went down the hill and made their precision GCA approaches to safe landing. The weather was dark and rainy but a world better than what they'd just left.

They taxied into the transient aircraft line and shut down. A bus took the pilots to the BOQ (bachelor officers quarters), where they changed into the uniform of the day. Once inside the Officers' Club next door, they immediately headed for the bar. For both of them, it had been a grueling, almost disastrous afternoon and evening. One of a group of pilots from a sister F-8 squadron, standing nearby, said, "Hey, T. R., we thought you guys were gone. Change your mind?"

There was silence for a moment, as the correct but dramatic answer would have taken too long to explain. Bobby Warren, he of the airplane-and-crash-truck-hopping fame, put everything in perspective.

"Oh, we just flew a routine round robin down to Iwakuni, shot a couple of touch-and-goes, and came back to Atsugi. Al Shiner decided to spend the night with some of the other guys."

T. R. wondered for a moment if they'd been on the same flight.

14   Everyone Out of the Pool!

Everyone knows that discipline forms the backbone of the military services. The "good order and discipline" phrase was one that General George Washington often used. How far does the "good order" edict go? You be the judge while I set the scene.

The year was 1952 at the Marine Corps Air Station, Kaneohe, on the Hawaiian Island of Oahu. The base had only recently been reopened after being closed at the end of World War II. The first jet squadron ever to be stationed in the Islands had arrived in September of that year, it being VMF-214, Pappy Boyington's Black Sheep Squadron.

Times were good (except for the Korean War, which was in progress). The weather was clear and pleasant, and the pilots of three sister marine fighter squadrons and VMF-214 were flying among the sparkling islands of the Hawaiian chain. One of the extracurricular activities, for whatever reason, was to take a dip in the Officers' Club swimming pool, with all of your clothes on. No one knew how it started, but just about every night one or more of the pilots would decide it was the "right stuff" thing to do, usually after hoisting a few during happy hour. Sometimes these celebrants were in the uniform of the day, but most of the time, they were in their fashionable slacks and aloha shirts.

Not surprisingly, a commanding officer's Official Directive was soon promulgated which read something like this: "To all Units Aboard: It has come to the attention of the Commanding Officer that certain personnel are entering the swimming pool improperly attired. This practice will cease immediately. Only bathing suits and other attire deemed appropriate for survival training will be worn. This Directive is effective immediately." Signed, Colonel So & So, Commanding. (I hesitate to use his real name, even today.)

Not strangely, this directive was basically ignored by the offending parties, and unauthorized late-night pool entries continued at an alarming rate. The good colonel—and he was a nice guy—decided that at the next Welcome Aboard Party (all officers and their ladies *will* attend), he would stand up and offer his official welcoming words to the newly arrived, and then inform all present that there would be no more "unauthorized pool entries," as he liked to call them. "Jumping into the pool with all of your clothes on" didn't sound official and certainly seemed much less dignified.

The gala Saturday night arrived. All the officers were resplendent in their dress whites, as were the ladies in their carefully chosen gowns. The colonel called for quiet, stopping the orchestra in midbar.

After a short welcoming address, he made the pronouncement regarding the improper use of the pool, which was just outside of the club ballroom.

"It is with some regret, but with firm commitment that I

must announce that the next person to enter one of our base swimming pools in improper attire, as spelled out clearly in my earlier Directive, will be subject to house arrest and to severe disciplinary action." As he let the words sink in around the room, the crowd grew totally silent. The quiet was short-lived, however, as the sound of the high diving board being sprung rumbled through the night. All eyes turned toward the windows, which were at eye level with the high board, just in time to see *Mrs.* Commanding Officer execute a perfect swan dive into the emerald green waters below—in her gorgeous sequined gown, with a pink orchid corsage.

A shaken and horrified colonel quickly stepped down from the podium and disappeared out the "O" Club's side entrance.

We never learned whether "house arrest" or "severe disciplinary action" was instituted, but it was several weeks before either the colonel or his champion-diver wife were seen at the Officers' Club.

15 A Midair Collision Can Ruin Your Whole Morning

Yuma, Arizona is well known for its climate, which is usually quite clear and warm—perhaps a little too warm in July and August but on 23 January 1969, very pleasant indeed. The visibility was proudly posted in the aerology briefing area at forty miles, *plus;* the climate was Chamber of Commerce perfect for a flight of four TA-4 Douglas Skyhawks.

Lt. Col. Marvin Garrison was a career marine with an impeccable military record, considered by all to be a superb aviator. He was the commanding officer of VMT-103, a training squadron with twenty-four brand-new aircraft. Their mission was to train replacement pilots for combat duty in Vietnam, where the conflict was now in full swing.

Following an 0530 briefing, the syllabus flight was scheduled to provide bombing and rocket practice. No live (explosive) munitions were involved; rather the armament consisted of eight 25-pound practice bombs with shotgun marker shells, which produced a small puff of white smoke

Three TA-4 Skyhawks, taxiing out for an early morning takeoff.
Garrison collection

upon impact. Additionally, each plane carried eight 2.75-inch air-to-ground rockets, also with dummy heads.

The Skyhawk was an attack aircraft, a two-seated jet. Interestingly (and importantly, as will be seen), all four back seats were empty on this training flight. Student aviators under instruction were not allowed to take up passengers, and Colonel Garrison's back seat was vacant only by chance because of the early hour of the predawn launch. Later in the day, it was customary for all the instructors' back seats to be filled.

The flight was designated as "Blue Flight," unimaginative perhaps but serviceable. The flight briefing conducted by Colonel Garrison was routine and thorough, covering all phases of the training mission, including emergency procedures, should they become necessary.

On Marv's wing as Blue Two was 1st Lt. Joe Fant, twenty-three, a native of Berkeley, California. Blue Three was 1st Lt. Robert Farns, also twenty-three, from Minot, North Dakota, who had been an All-Conference basketball player at UCLA. Tail-end Charlie as Blue Four was J. D. Lawson, twenty-four, from Canterbury Hill, Tops Field, Massachusetts.

The four aircraft taxied out to the duty runway from their squadron flight line.

"Yuma Tower, this is Blue Lead"—the tactical call sign—"in Sierra Delta Zero One with four TA-4's; request taxi, time and altimeter."

"Roger, Sierra Delta Zero One"—the aircraft side number—"your flight cleared as Tactical Blue Flight for takeoff and to proceed to restricted area 2501. Time is 0629, altimeter setting, 29.94. Report to Rocket Range Two on 332.3—call leaving field boundaries."

"Affirmative, Tower." Marv then led the flight on to the duty runway for individual takeoffs. As they made their running rendezvous and joined up, he signaled for a UHF radio frequency change as the four gleaming, shiny new jets climbed westward in perfect formation. Their assigned altitude en route to the target area was eight thousand feet, the height from which they would make their sixteen individual bombing and rocket runs. It was 0640. The desert floor was still dark; the sun was just coming up above the curved horizon.

After locating the designated target area and observation posts (spotting towers) and after checking in with "Desert Rats" (the ground parties' self-designated call sign), Blue Flight was cleared to commence eight bombing runs. Marv wondered momentarily why the spotters had switched call signs from their official Navy "Rocket Range Two" call sign. But a glance at the bleak sand and sage brush surroundings satisfied any doubt in his mind.

"Blue Lead, rolling in on first run." This was a required radio transmission, along with an "off target" call as each pilot pulled up and off the target, which was a series of concentric circles, the center one being fifty feet in diameter.

"Blue Leader, your hit, six o'clock, ten feet," this from Desert Rat. Not bad, Marv thought, for the first run.

The mission proceeded—eight bombing runs from eight thousand feet, 45-degree dive, pull out left, four and a half G's, climb back up to the perch—keeping eyes peeled for the other three planes. Blue Lead after the eight runs had six bulls along with two hits just outside the inner circle. The young lieutenants were not quite as accurate, averaging ninety to a hundred feet from the center circle—not that they were expected to be "aces" on their early bombing runs. But that was their mission: to learn, train, and become proficient *before* it would be time to drop 500- and 1,000-pounders with more serious thoughts in mind.

"Blue Flight, switch to rockets, same direction of runs. And remember to call both rolling in and off target. We'll stay in a left-hand pattern. Break . . . break . . . Desert Rat, Blue Leader is in first rocket run."

The runs continued, with each pilot improving his accuracy as the mission proceeded. As briefed, the pilots would call off the target, check armament switches safe, and on the last run indicate their fuel state (e.g., 2,500 lbs. would be "two point five"), and end with "Tally-ho" (meaning, "I have the flight in sight").

"This is Blue Lead. Last run, rolling in." A few seconds later: "Blue Lead is off target, all switches safe, state two point six. We'll rendezvous left-hand orbit at three thousand feet—west of the target. We've got some cloud cover that's moved in. Acknowledge. Over."

"This is Dash Two. Roger. Rolling in."

"Dash Three, Roger."

"Dash Four, Roger," Another pause, and then some thirty seconds later:

"Dash Two off, switches safe, two point five. Tally-ho."

"Dash Three off, switches safe, two point three. Tally-ho."

There was no off-target call from Blue Four.

"Blue Four, this is Blue Lead. Do you have the flight in sight?" No response. By this time, Numbers Two and Three were joined up and flying a loose but comfortable free cruise wing position.

"Two and Three, do either of you have Four in sight?"

Before either wingman could answer, the missing TA-4 showed up dramatically—slamming into the lead aircraft, slicing it in two, exactly thirty-six inches behind the front cockpit, where another pilot or passenger would have been sitting.

Marv's cockpit immediately filled with flames and smoke. He was now flying a tailless airplane. Actually, he was now riding as a *passenger* in a tailless airplane. The violent tumbling with attendant high G forces made it extremely difficult for the pilot to eject. He remembered later:

"It took me several attempts to grasp the ejection face curtain handle. Each time I'd just about get a hold of it, I'd get slammed against the sides of the canopy and have to let go. I knew there were only a few seconds left." He felt the intense heat from the burning JP-5 fuel through his flight clothing and wondered if being burned alive would be quick. He knew it would be painful.

With precious little altitude remaining, Marv made one final desperate grab and pulled the ejection curtain. With a loud bang and a whoosh, he was finally clear of the flaming jet. He was still in the soup, though, because the aircraft was upside down when he ejected. He was now plunging straight down toward the ground, using up what little time remained for pulling the rip cord and opening his chute. Lady Luck intervened at this moment and the parachute snapped open with a bone-shattering jerk. From three hundred knots to a motionless standstill position hanging in midair, the everlovin' (Marv's words) Navy's automatic, sequentially opening device had saved his life. He swung for only half an arc and landed unceremoniously but feet first into a recently plowed bean field. Somewhere Marv's Guardian Angel wiped her brow.

After Blue Four had collided with his flight leader, his right wing cutting the other jet in half, the Skyhawk was not flying very well. However, Lieutenant Lawson was somewhat luckier than Marv in that his aircraft did not catch fire. As the Skyhawk flopped over and over, with only half a wing, Blue Four pulled his face curtain, ejected *uneventfully*—to use the oxymoronic military phrase—and landed after five or ten swings in another bean field several miles away. He didn't have a scratch.

The morning's routine four-plane training flight was no longer routine, with half of the pilots standing on the ground, alive, and watching the burning wrecks of their two Skyhawks.

Overhead, Blue Two was now Flight Leader (as prebriefed), and he immediately set about handling the emergencies. Yuma Control Tower was notified, and the Air-Sea Rescue Helicopter was launched. Blue Three was dispatched to fly low and slow over the crash sites to locate, if possible, the two pilots.

Lt. Lawson was found almost at once, not far from his crashed aircraft, and waved that he was OK. Marv was spotted several minutes later, also near his burning jet—actually, only the front half of it. The empennage, or tail portion, was a good half-mile away but not on fire. Blue Leader was observed by the low flying TA-4 in Blue Three to be standing on the bank of an irrigation canal, hands on hips, vehemently shaking his head. The colonel was somewhat upset. Fortunately, Lieutenant Lawson was a safe distance away.

In about forty minutes the Yuma Air Station SAR helo picked up the two ejectees and delivered them to the station hospital for their mandatory physical checkups. Neither was

VMT-103's commanding officer entering TA-4, 1969. The Nomex flight suit prevented him from being seriously burned. *Garrison collection*

seriously hurt, although Marv had been burned on the back of his neck. He had survived the airborne inferno mainly because he was wearing a Nomex flight suit, Nomex gloves, and even Nomex underwear—all designed to be fireproof.

The subsequent accident investigation revealed that Blue Four, during his pullout on the last rocket firing run, had inadvertently let his radio cord become unplugged, probably due to the four-and-a-half-G pullout forces. As he attempted to reattach the cord connection, he'd overshot the other three rendezvousing aircraft, having forgotten to reduce power. Lieutenant Lawson then zoomed up above the flight at a much higher speed than the prebriefed three hundred knots for joining up. He'd hastily closed the throttle and deployed speed brakes to slow down. From several thousand feet now above the flight, his aircraft suddenly snap rolled into a spin and hurtled down vertically, out of control, striking the flight leader's aircraft. Inattention for only a moment had almost cost the lives of two Marine pilots.

Near the town of El Centro witnesses on the ground had observed the midair collision and the two crashed jets. One was a foreman in charge of a Mexican working crew who had heard a loud explosion—the sound of the two jets colliding—but by the time he located the direction and the cause of the noise, both aircraft had already crashed. The reflective glint of Marv's collapsing white parachute canopy was all he could see, as it had all happened so quickly and so near to the ground (starting at only three thousand feet altitude). But one Latino in the work party had actually seen the entire scene, from impact to fireball to Marv's last-minute ejection. His statement as it appeared on the navy's official accident investigation report read:

"I see the planes. They run together. Big fireball. Then little man come out bottom of fireball. I run."

Epilogue

Col. Marv Garrison, USMC, Ret., says that he often relives the experience and realizes how lucky he was to survive the midair collision that morning—which came so very close to ruining his entire day.

First Lieutenant Lawson was given an Aviator's Disposition Board, where his fitness to continue flying was at issue. The board gave him another chance, largely on the recommendation given by Blue Leader. Lieutenant Lawson turned out to be an excellent pilot and Marine Corps officer. Sadly, he was killed a year later in Vietnam by enemy ground fire in an A-4 Skyhawk.

16 Nothing Can Stop the Army Air Corps

In 1943 during World War II, an American bomber group was stationed at an airfield on the outskirts of London. They were highly trained B-17 pilots and somewhat proud of their role—that of saving England. The pilots had a good deal, and they knew it. So did the pubs, the townspeople, and, of course, the local girls.

One day there was some grim news: An American fighter group was moving into their area at a nearby airfield. The bomber pilots plotted in their club at night for a week, seeking a suitable welcome for the "Fighter Jocks." Finally, they had it.

At high noon on a rarely beautiful English day, all hands at the fighter group's airfield peered aloft as a low-flying B-17 made several low passes across their tarmac. Slowly the bomb bay doors opened and a large dark object came hurtling down. A direct hit was scored on the shiny new white concrete apron just in front of Field Operations. The object turned out to be a 300-pound bag of cow manure. When dropped from an altitude of a thousand feet, it had not only made its mark, it had splattered magnificently.

Back at the B-17 base, the bomber boys were ecstatic that evening in their club. The perpetrators had to tell and retell their mission, each time to an appreciative and applauding audience. Finally, someone in the back of the room said: "Wonder what they'll think up in return."

It was a good question, and no one could come close to a suggestion of how the "manure caper" could be topped. For three long days and nights, the entire bomber group waited with bated breath. Finally, on the fourth day at the bomber group's evening muster, a small liaison plane was observed heading directly toward their airfield. Obviously, this must be a retaliatory raid from the Fighter Boys. Many took cover, not knowing what to expect.

After several very slow and deliberate turns, the small plane waggled its wings and a small object with a white streamer attached floated to the tarmac below. Gingerly, with great caution, an airman retrieved the object. Closer examination revealed no booby trap, only an old flying boot. Further search revealed a note securely fastened inside the boot. It read:

"To the 403rd bomber group: It is with our deepest regret that the officers and men of the 33rd Fighter Group must report that your Commanding Officer fell to his death at our airfield three days ago."

17 Fun over Afghanistan

H e'd been catapulted off the flight deck of the USS *Stennis* at "O-dark hundred," in his words. It was 1:30 A.M., somewhere in the North Arabian Sea. Lt. Cdr. Anthony Wright from Virginia Beach, Virginia, was not on vacation, as his squadron mates liked to say, but on a close air support mission, heavily loaded with two 1,000-pound bombs. The pilot, a member of the "Argonauts" of Strike Fighter Squadron VFA-147, was well qualified, with over two thousand hours in type (F/A-18) and 570 arrested carrier landings. It was mid-January, almost four months after 11 September 2001.

His single-seat F/A-18 Hornet was (and is) the U.S. Navy's first line fighter and attack aircraft. Flying his wing and tucked in closely was his wingman, Lt. Gregory Brown of Juneau, Alaska. Only their faint wing lights showed as they circled above the barren valleys northeast of Kandahar, halfway to Kabul, the present capital of Afghanistan. Their assigned time on station was to be six hours, with a scheduled recovery time of 0730. Each pilot knew, heading out, that no matter how exciting their combat mission might be, the dramatic climax to the flight was always going to be the trap (landing) aboard the pitching, angled carrier deck. Pilot skill was a dominant factor, but Lady Luck sometimes played a role, too.

To spend six hours in the cramped cockpit requires great stamina, entailing as it does a high tolerance for boredom, exceptional bladder control, and the reserve energy for an occasional burst of frenetic effort as ground targets are identified and attacked. Orders would be issued by airborne command controllers from other circling aircraft in conjunction with ground command posts.

This entire process is made possible by airborne filling stations that strongly resemble civilian DC-10s, possibly because they are DC-10s configured as tankers. These USAF aircraft, called KC-10s (to confuse the enemy, as Lt. Cdr. Wright says) carry many tons of jet fuel and have a single refueling hose with a basket-looking device at the end into which the jet's refueling probe is inserted. (The pilots' more colorful terms are thoughtfully omitted here.)

Lt. Cdr. Wright's flight customarily tanked (refueled) while orbiting at twenty-five thousand feet—first at 0215, then at 0330 and again at 0600. The point is to maintain a near full fuel state, in case a hot target should turn up suddenly. The average temperature at that altitude is minus 40 degrees Fahrenheit. For the pilot, that fact, while interesting, has little practical effect because of the jet fighter's cockpit pressurization and very effective heater. Except for the leg room and lavatory facilities, the pilot's comfort level was roughly similar to that of a commercial DC-10 en route to Somewhere, USA.

At 0600, cruising at his assigned air speed of 300 mph, Lt. Cdr. Wright began topping off his fuel per schedule. Suddenly, the DC-10 airliner similarities ended. The plugged-in refueling hose ripped apart without warning, leaving approximately eight feet of hose flailing about the cockpit canopy. The basket was still attached to the fighter jet's fueling probe, and the rubberized hose had separated at a brass connector fitting. The brass connector weighed about ten pounds and in the pilot's exact words, "was beating the living hell out of my airplane. This is gonna be bad, real bad. After twenty or so violent whacks, the canopy gave up the ghost. I never thought what a shattering canopy would sound like, until then, of course. It sounded just like when you go through a plate glass window. All this in a heartbeat."

The acrylic canopy exploded outwardly because of the pressurized cockpit. This was good. But now the pilot was riding in a 300-mile-an-hour wind at 40 degrees below zero. The chill factor was off the page. He was sitting in an icy convertible with the top down.

"The tanker," Wright went on to say "was last seen turning for the Southeast, spewing gas all over the place and its pilot spewing words over the radio—like it was something *I'd* done. Thought about squaring away *those* air force guys but it wasn't the time."

After extending his dive brake to reduce speed, the pilot hunkered down as far as possible to avoid the icy blast. He then turned up the cockpit heater to full blast, keeping his feet "warm and toasty but everything above that was in the chilly zone"—again, his words. Once slowed to a "reasonable" speed of 250 mph, Wright began to plot his return to earth. He'd have to fly across Afghanistan low and slow to reach the carrier some 650 miles away. He'd be flying the perfect profile, or route, that the enemy antiaircraft gunners would love, and, once safely through that ordeal, he was supposed to land on a carrier. The idea of a carrier landing in his open-air vehicle was not appealing. In fact, it wasn't just risky, it was stupid.

Upon rejecting this chainsaw-mentality notion, he decided to land instead at JBAD, a forward operating base less than an hour away. As Wright eyed the razor-sharp remnants of the canopy sticking up on both sides of the cockpit, Lieutenant Brown came up on the radio.

"Hey, can you reach out and grab that thing . . . pull it in?"

Wright's exasperation in response wasn't visible behind his visor and oxygen mask, but came through loud and clear on the radio.

"Stick my arm out into that wind? Get it blasted back and thrashed on the glass shards everywhere? Have you lost your mind?"

"Oh, yeah, guess it's kinda windy," the wingman responded.

"It's strange, the thoughts you have sometimes," Wright remembers. "First, sitting too close to the display screen on the instrument panel was supposed to be bad on the eyes." (He's facing a possible death situation and worrying about eye strain?) Another thought was a bit more realistic. He radioed his wingman, "The Air Force at JBAD is going to love me when I tell them about the two 1,000-pounders I'm bringing them." Then he told the carrier not to expect him back just yet.

They landed at the air force field at 0710 without further incident.

At 1100 hours, a maintenance team from the *Stennis*, headed by Chief Aviation Electronics Technician Robert Palmer, arrived by a C-2 transport aircraft. In four hours they had replaced the disintegrated canopy and patched the numerous holes with 300-mile-an-hour tape. Wright was ordered by his commanding officer to "stay down and rest" before flying again. He did so gladly after his wingman, Lieutenant Brown, refueled and returned to the *Stennis*.

Resting up at the airfield, Wright learned shortly that the local entertainment in the form of Drew Carey and Joan Jett had just left, and that Shania Twain was due the next day. His USAF accommodations were comfortable, and the proficient navy maintenance personnel who had reassembled his aircraft were also well treated, sharing similar air-conditioned lodging. Things were getting back to normal.

At sunrise the patched-up F/A-18 took off for the carrier, low and fast, "due to the locals with poor attitudes and guns," Wright said. The C-2 aircraft followed shortly thereafter with the tech personnel. After an uneventful tanking en route, Wright flew smoothly toward the *Stennis*—until at about a one mile final on his landing approach, when a hydraulic pressure warning light flashed on. Suddenly his aileron control "went bonkers" (his words). Hitting a reset button regained control momentarily. Immediately another caution light illuminated, and he had lost one aileron, one rudder (of two), and half of his horizontal stabilizer. The reset button was pushed again, but adequate flight control was in doubt.

"When the ailerons failed again, I realized I needed to get aboard on the first pass. Man, first I miss Shania and now this! I got it aboard only because the F/A-18 Hornet is a fantastic jet."

He landed safely, saving the airplane. Postflight inspection revealed a broken hydraulic pump shaft, meaning that he had had only minutes of controlled flight remaining. His commanding officer, Cdr. Brick Imerman, was waiting for him with congratulations on all fronts. Wright, along with his navy maintenance crew, had performed their duties in an exemplary manner. Yes, it was the "right stuff," all the way.

As Wright told his fellow pilots that evening in their ready room, "Just another ho-hum fun day over Afghanistan."

Epilogue

Lt. Commander Wright told me this story via e-mail from his quarters on the *Stennis*. After completing his Afghanistan tour, he returned to San Diego in July 2002 and is now stationed at NAS Lemoore, California. At this writing he is still a member of the VFA-147 Argonauts.

As proud as I am to have been a combat carrier fighter pilot and part of naval aviation for twenty-five years, this true story makes me even prouder.

18 The Midnight Pound Cake Helicopter Rescue

In the early days of rotary wing flying, the helicopter was envisioned as a better and quicker means of rescuing downed airmen, stranded hikers, and seriously injured motorists. Since then, both civilian and particularly the military uses of the helicopter have been expanded tremendously. The armed forces' main role for helicopters now involves troop carrying, resupplying missions, and—the most attention-getting of all—the functions of attack or gunship types, such as the Apache and the Huey Cobra.

The point, of course, is that helicopters are not to be taken lightly; they are serious machines, even if not waging war. I have a story for you about a daring night mission over the swamps of the Marine Corps's Camp Lejeune, N.C., that removes all doubt. I was the pilot, and it certainly would have removed mine if I'd had any.

In the early fall of 1956 our Marine Observation Squadron (VMO-1) had just received some brand new helicopters, the

Kaman-built HOK-1, a four-place machine. Its assigned missions were observation, liaison, special reconnaissance insertions, minimal resupply (with a maximum passenger payload of only about six hundred pounds), and most importantly, rescue operations.

The HOK-1 had an external hoist for rescue purposes. A crewman would operate the three-hundred-foot cable to which a rescue "collar" was attached. A wire stretcher, or litter, could also be attached, theoretically, but the very small cabin space made such a maneuver impractical. Hence, all of the rescue training was done with the tried-and-true "horse collar."

A word about this new machine. It sported, if that's the word, a four-bladed, counter-rotating, intersecting rotor system. Kaman Aircraft, in an effort to eliminate the twenty- to twenty-five-percent loss of power due to torque found in all tail-rotored helicopters, had two blades rotating in one direction and another two in the opposite direction, hence the "counter-rotating" action. There were some detractors who described the helo as resembling an "infuriated palm tree." Others referred to the HOK-1 as "a candle without a wick." Those of us who flew it just figured it was a "challenge."

One of the problems from the pilots' point of view was that in flight it shook quite a bit. It didn't exactly loosen your fillings, but it made reading the engine and flight instruments very difficult. Now, this isn't a big deal *except* when flying in bad weather, or at night, which we had to do. But the night operations were carefully scheduled during favorable weather and moonlight conditions. Reference lights, such as runway lighting, city lights, and almost any highway with automobile lights would be sufficient to keep the pilot in touch with his aircraft's attitude in reference to the horizon—very important. The reader may remember the tragic accident that took the lives of John F. Kennedy, Jr. and his two passengers. He had lost his reference to the horizon at dusk.

Two more important items need to be emphasized here. First, the HOK-1 had two separate landing lights with an effective range of about two hundred feet. The second item that the reader must be aware of is the "dead man's curve." Emergency landings are accomplished in helicopters by autorotating. For example, if you're tooling along at almost any reasonable altitude, a hundred to five hundred feet or more, and the engine quits . . . not to worry. You just lower the collective lever, which reduces the angle of attack on all four rotor blades simultaneously, like nosing over in a fixed-wing aircraft. Now both types are in the gliding mode. With the helicopter there is residual lift built up as the machine is descending while the pilot looks for a suitable spot to land. (Over the ocean, of course, you're screwed, to use official pilot talk.) The pilot then executes a flare just above the ground, and using the rotor system's momentum, raises the collective lever, allowing the helicopter to lightly touch down, certainly to the relief of all aboard. This maneuver is routinely practiced by all helo pilots and is part of their training syllabus.

But what if you're *hovering* at, say two hundred feet? You have no forward speed. Then you are, unfortunately, smack in the middle of the "deadman's curve." You don't have enough altitude to push over, regain forward speed (and rotor lift) to enter a controlled autorotation maneuver. The result is not good (for comparable outcome, see helicopter-over-water situation). A crash, usually fatal, occurs.

In essence, this is what killed Francis Gary Powers, the famous U-2 pilot, some years ago, while flying a traffic-watch helicopter near Los Angeles. When an engine failure occurs, you must reduce the collective pitch immediately and nose over to a gliding mode; apparently he did not. Thus, even to the uneducated, the solution is patently obvious: Stay out of the "dead man's curve." Speaking for all helicopter pilots everywhere, I will say, "We always try to."

On the plus side of the HOK-1's performance envelope, it was very easy to fly, although the pilot could never take both hands off the controls for very long. Perhaps its biggest plus was a very reliable engine. I don't recall anyone having an engine failure in flight. If there were any, they didn't happen on my watch.

In October, 1956 I was living in government quarters with my family on the base at Camp Lejeune. As I remember, my wife and I were watching the Nat King Cole show on TV. At around 9:00 P.M. the telephone rang. It was our squadron's commanding officer, Lt. Col. Paul Pankhurst.

"Captain Tooker, please," he'd said.

"Speaking, Sir," I'd replied, recognizing the colonel's voice immediately.

"Don, I've just had a call from the air station's staff duty officer. We've been requested to provide an emergency air-evac out in that area where we've been dropping those Recon guys." Inserting the Recon Teams was always a challenge to all of us. We often dropped them in heavily wooded forests, along rivers, and, in this case, into some very unpleasant swamp areas.

"Apparently they've got a marine in critical condition, too far out to reach him by vehicle, I guess. You've got the most time in the HOK. What do you think? Can you take it? I know it's blacker than hell out tonight."

"Yes, Sir, I'll get right on it. It'll take me about thirty-five minutes to drive out to squadron. Could you alert our duty officer to preflight a bird and, oh yes, if we can locate Staff Sergeant Chester, he has the most experience with rescue hoist operations. I won't be taking a copilot; we'll need the extra lifting power." I hoped I'd made the right decision there.

"Fine, Don, I knew I could count on you. We'll have everything set when you get there." A long pause, then, "Be careful now, don't do anything foolish."

I mumbled a soft "Yes, Sir," thinking at the time that the whole damned mission fell into the heart of the "foolish" category. Flying the HOK around lighted cities and airfields was one thing, but unless the swamps were now ablaze with lights and beacons, it could be a long night. When I said goodbye to the wife on my way out the door, she'd had that "You *do* know what you're doing?" look. I sure hoped I did.

As I drove along toward squadron, I remembered again what the Marine Corps Recon guys did for a living. Much like the Navy Seals of today, their missions included being dropped secretly behind enemy lines. Around home base they played the aggressor role. They would attempt to sneak up on the good guy marines and harass, capture or otherwise mess up their training exercises. They lived mostly on C rations, stealth, and high esprit de corps.

The squadron hangar was lit up and a HOK was sitting on the flight line with a ready look, if helicopters can ever look ready. The best news of all was that Staff Sergeant Chester was there and already in his flight suit. What little

I knew about rescue hoisting procedures I'd learned from him. He was a real pro.

My confidence level was full to the brim now, as only a former fighter pilot, now rescue helicopter pilot, could be. Having Chester along didn't hurt either.

"She's all set, Captain. I've checked everything, including the hoist mechanisms. We got a copilot coming?"

"No, Sarge, I decided we might be too heavy if our rescuee turns out to be a heavyweight. Murphy's Law says he'll probably weigh three hundred pounds."

Sergeant Chester ignored my attempt at levity and set about stowing extra flashlights and some water while I quickly changed into my flight gear.

A call to the staff duty officer produced the approximate map coordinates of the evacuee along with the ground unit's radio frequency. The Recon boys were to shine their combined flashlights vertically when we were in their vicinity. Their one vehicle, whatever it was, would supply additional light for a homing source. The estimated ground distance to their location was about thirty-five to forty miles due north, and they were in an area surrounded by swamp—a very dark swamp.

"Skipper, what's the condition of the victim?" Sergeant Chester had asked. (Marine captains are often called "Skipper.")

"Just critical, was the only thing Colonel Pankhurst said, whatever that means. Probably a broken leg, who knows. Maybe he just wants to come back to the base for the evening movie." This time I got a brief laugh from my hoist operator.

After about a half-hour of flying, we reached the general area of the pickup. It was 10:45 and there was no moon. I'd kept an eye on some distant lights that provided some measure of reference to the almost invisible horizon. The artificial horizon gyro instrument was barely readable in the dim cockpit lighting. Even though my night vision was finally accommodating, I knew the real test would come when hovering over our intended rescuee. The chopper would vibrate so much that the instruments would become useless. And there was one other item of concern: We would be in the heart of the "dead man's curve."

"Rescue helicopter, this is Bravo Three. We hear you. Do you read me, over?"

"That's affirmative," I replied.

"Roger, Rescue Chopper, you're above us to the east. Come west, due west. We'll blink the jeep's lights."

We flew west as directed for several minutes but with no sighting.

"You see anything, Sarge?" I asked.

"No, Sir, nothing yet. The heavy undergrowth blocks out everything."

"Rescue Chopper, Bravo Three. You just flew over us, about a football field to the south." I was glad the Recon boys didn't tell me in meters.

"OK, Bravo Three, I'll start a slow orbit to the left, moving north. I'll use half a football field in the orbit." Silence for a moment, then:

"I got 'em, Sir, about three o'clock low." The sergeant had the best eyes, but *he* didn't have to fly the plane.

"OK, Bravo Three, we've got your position spotted. What's the situation with your man?"

"Roger, our corpsman is pretty sure Private O'Brien has acute appendicitis. He's afraid it's going to rupture. Can you pick him up, over?"

"That's a Roger," I responded. "But it's going to be difficult. I'll need your help. First, put those headlights on bright beam, then try to place the flashlight guys at the four corners of a square with the evacuee in the center. You copy that, Bravo Three?" Several moments went by as I imagined the ground control man issuing orders.

"Roger, Rescue Chopper. Can do. But I can't promise a perfect square. The terrain down here is uncertain. Too much swamp, too little road."

"OK, I understand. We'll be lowering the cable in a moment. It has a horse collar, and your man has to put his head, shoulders, and arms through it. The *minute* he's in tight, tell me. I can't hover precisely with so few reference points. You understand?"

"Affirmative," Bravo Three acknowledged.

"Chester, you'll be my eyes. Keep me honest. I should be able to hold altitude but you'll have to control our drift."

"No sweat, Skipper." His vote of confidence did little to reduce my now sweaty-palms condition. We were on the hairy side of the rescue mission, and both of us knew it. If we got the guy in the collar and suddenly moved in any direction, we'd be dragging him through some unfriendly Carolina scrub pine trees. The possibility of an engine failure was simply not considered.

From Bravo Three: "Your horse collar is about fifty feet to the left, Rescue Chopper, and too high." I took a quick glance at the altimeter. It revealed a blurry nothing. We moved left then right, then up and too far down. I was pretty much all over the night sky.

"Down a hair, Skipper, and if you can hold it right there, I'll try to get him in the collar."

With the sergeant hoisting, Bravo Three directing, and me struggling at the vibrating controls for what seemed forever, we all finally heard the welcome cry:

"He's in. Hoist away!" I cranked on the power as the sergeant began to hoist in the cable and all of a sudden we had Private O'Brien making like the Flying Nun, airborne over the swamp, moving faster than he probably ever had been in his life. Several minutes later, Sergeant Chester pulled him safely into the cabin as we headed for the barn, in this case the Naval Hospital helo pad at Camp Lejeune. I radioed ahead to the staff duty officer to have a doctor meet our helicopter and that we had a marine aboard with a possible life-threatening emergency.

We set down on the well-lit landing zone and were met by a doctor, two corpsmen with a stretcher, and a nurse. Once relieved of our human cargo, we departed for our squadron flight line. Glancing at my watch, I noted it was exactly midnight.

The family was asleep when I finally got home. It took at least an hour for the excitement of the evening to die down. Somewhere around 2:00 A.M. I finally drifted off.

"Good flight, dear?" my wife had asked next morning.

"Yeah. We picked up a young marine way out in the boonies. Nothing we couldn't handle. Worked with that Sergeant Chester I told you about." I figured she didn't need to know how close to the edge we'd been operating.

On my way to work the next morning, albeit a couple of hours later than usual, I decided to stop by the base hospital and see how my "patient" was doing. I had not been able to speak to him on the way back from the swamp pickup event.

"Sorry, Captain," the duty chief said: "We have no record of any Private O'Brien being admitted."

I explained the previous night's excitement, leaving out the personal tension and degree of difficulty involved, which was a *ten* on a scale of ten. He was understanding and left in search of further information. Several minutes later he returned with a nurse who looked like the one who had met our helicopter at the hospital landing pad.

"This is Lieutenant Knowler. She was on duty last night, Captain," the navy chief said.

"I was trying to find out how Private O'Brien is doing, I think that was his name. I was the rescue helo pilot." She looked at me long and hard and then smiled slightly.

"Well, Captain, we got him into ER, where we learned he'd eaten nothing but cheese crackers and pound cake for four days—all without a B.M. Apparently, he didn't care for anything else offered in his C rations menu. After an enema or two, he was fine, so we released him for full duty this morning."

Words failed me. Initially I was relieved, then a little flabbergasted, ending up being thoroughly torqued off! The toughest rescue mission of my life, and all that was really needed was a damned bowel movement.

I reported the incident to the colonel, who felt exactly as I did—relieved and then angry. He'd realized the extreme risk involved in our mission, and I just didn't have the heart to let Sergeant Chester in on the truth. He'd risked his life as I had, doing his job with great professionalism.

You never know for sure when an emergency pops up whether it might be at the call of duty—or at the call of nature.

19 I Took the Monotony out of Commuting

In 1945, just after the end of World War II, I read an article in the Sunday *Los Angeles Times* that said or implied that in twenty-five years most people would be going to work in their own airplanes. There were several pictures showing how, with convertible car-planes, in thirty-eight seconds you could snap the wings and rudder onto the family car, point yourself into the wind, and presto! you'd be winging your way to work, far above the bumper-to-bumper traffic jams below.

Well, twenty-three years passed, and in 1968, when I retired from the Marine Corps and went to work for a large aerospace firm, I commuted to work by air while "most people" still jammed the freeways below. Five days a week, rain or shine, in sickness and in health, you could look up and see me in my little Cessna Commuter making like Charles Lindbergh. Of course, I realize that it took some courage for him to fly over all that water, but at least he didn't have to dodge all those other lightplanes, airliners, and traffic helicopters. Although most people were still driving, I was never alone up there. Lord, it was like a summer Sunday at Disneyland every day.

Here in the Los Angeles area, where the weather usually is good, motorists utilize a crowded freeway system. Ten million cars all try to take their owners to work between 6:00 and 9:00 A.M. In the three years of commuting I saw more auto accidents, stalled busses, and overturned tomato trucks than I ever thought possible. The time that two thousand chickens got loose on the Hollywood Freeway Interchange is still very memorable. And if predictions of the land developers hold true—that the entire country is moving to California in the next ten years—it should make today's congestion look like the North Pole in the off season.

Still, it was not an easy decision to commute by air in my own airplane. You don't purchase an $8,000 item casually on the chance that maybe it'll be a good deal. I'm an organized guy, operating with an overall plan. All my suits are hung in the closet facing the same direction. And when I die, my wife inherits 51 percent of U.S. Steel, the Queen Mary, and all the proceeds from Sunny Tufts' old movies. I wanted to fly, and I had a pretty good argument to support the idea.

To begin with, we'd purchased a beautiful home in Oceanside, California, right on the water. You could walk out the back door, cross the sand, and wade into the Pacific Ocean. The house was what every family dreams about and can't possibly afford. Unfortunately, the job opportunities in the adjoining small towns were nil. My local employment options were so few that I began to covet my son's paper route. However, I finally accepted an excellent position with Lockheed at a site north of Los Angeles in Van Nuys.

Now the problem was transportation, since our cherished

house was 120 miles to the south. It meant three hours of driving each way during rush-hour traffic at its worst. I would become one of the ten million. Since we weren't about to move from the beach location and needed a job to continue eating and to keep our four kids in school, something had to give.

A friend suggested just coming home on the weekends, as some workers did, but I figured I could go back into the Marine Corps for another twenty-five years perhaps and see more of my family than that. The solution became obvious.

My suggestion to my wife that night at dinner that we buy an airplane was met by a hotbed of indifference. She didn't see any need to erase an already fading savings program (buying a new house can do that). Still, she had no better suggestion. It finally boiled down to the job *and* the airplane, or no job and no airplane. Besides, I've always made the real decisions in the family: whether China should be allowed to join the U.N., what to do about the earth's ozone layer, etc. I've let her handle the day-to-day stuff: selling or buying a home, adopting a child, education for the kids, etc. And I wanted to fly.

One week later I became the proud owner of a two-place maroon-and-white Cessna 150, appropriately called the "Commuter." It cruised along at a mean 120 miles an hour, and after only five years it would be all mine. It was a 1967 model and almost new. I'd considered buying several older and less expensive planes, but the predictably higher maintenance costs and reliability factors negated this. The daily trips across the heart of the Los Angeles basin, with its wall-to-wall houses, gave a reliable engine number one priority.

The Cessna 150 Commuter awaits its daily riders at the Oceanside Municipal Airport in Southern California.

A forced landing into someone's swimming pool would be really embarrassing.

We did save some money on flying lessons, as I'd logged over seven thousand hours of flying time as a Marine Corps pilot (in another life) in everything from open cockpit flying to swept-wing supersonic jets, not to mention helicopters. True, the Cessna wasn't supersonic, quite, but I felt confident that I could handle the majority of its one hundred horses.

My first day at work was a real Pearl Harbor. Proud and loaded with confidence, I had driven to the small Oceanside Airport where my newly purchased transportation awaited. I remember thinking it was great to be starting out on a second career at age forty-two. As a prospective "captain of industry" I couldn't keep thoughts of bigger and faster planes, achievable in a few years, from running through my head. Upon arriving at the airport, though, a new problem arose. I couldn't find the airplane. A pea-soup fog had rolled in and obscured the airport valley, the runway, everything! Just locating the little Cessna was about as difficult as explaining to my six-year-old son how clams go to the bathroom. By the time I found it, a call from the airport's hot line to the FAA Flight Service in San Diego had revealed that all the coastal airports from Mexico to Los Angeles were closed (fogged in). Nothing was flying. However, the airport in Van Nuys, which was located on the other side of the Los Angeles hills, was marginally open. But it required an instrument approach.

A decision was made. After filing an instrument flight plan with San Diego Departure Control, I pushed my new bird out to the end of the runway. If I couldn't even get there on the first day of work, the boss, no matter how great and understanding a guy he might be, could perhaps become a little apprehensive about his new worker.

I started the engine, warmed it up, turned on the radio, and wished desperately that I hadn't lost that St. Christopher's medal back in the seventh grade. And so, after almost twenty-five years of military flying, three wars, and some rather near misses, I opened the throttle for the most difficult takeoff of my life.

In preparation for the takeoff, I had lined up the nose wheel right on the center of the white line. As takeoff speed was building, I looked away from the guiding earthbound white line and transitioned to the instrumented gyros, which reminded me that straight ahead was mandatory (there being steep hills on both sides of the runway) and that I would do well to observe the proper aircraft attitude. At seventy miles an hour I pulled back on the yoke and climbed into the milk-bottle sky. Never had anyone followed his instruments more carefully. Like a youngster on a driver's education lesson, I cautiously banked and headed toward the first radio navigational aid. It looked like the beginning of a long day. At two thousand feet we broke out into the bright sunshine. Once "on top," the old salty composure was regained, and my voice soon came back down to its normal radio-announcer tones. The air traffic controllers were all very helpful. Why not? Seven Nine Sierra was the only lightplane airborne in Southern California that morning. Even the airliners were being diverted into Ontario and other fields farther inland.

It turned out, however, to be a lovely flight. The sky was crystal-clear blue, and the solid fog bank below glistened like newly fallen snow. While the scenery was indeed picturesque, other thoughts marred my pseudo contentment. If the engine quit, I'd make the front pages, depending on where I crashed. Additionally, the destination weather was, as reported, "marginal." I thought about not having a parachute, but further introspection revealed that I was too much of a cheapskate to ever bail out of an $8,000 investment.

One hour later we (the Cessna and I) made a flawless instrument approach to the Van Nuys Airport. When the field had finally come into sight, I coolly switched to the control tower frequency and received clearance to land. The fact that I had landed on the taxiway instead of the duty runway was a little disconcerting, but the tower operators were very understanding. They had a lot of green, inexperienced pilots flying out of their airport. Of course, they hadn't known that they were dealing with a veteran Marine fighter pilot with thousands of flying hours—on his first day to work. But I was not late, and the boss was pleased that his dedicated new worker had taken the trouble to be there on time.

"Good flight, Don?" he had asked casually.

"Yes sir, real nice. No problem." Fortunately my damp armpits didn't divulge any of the earlier flying difficulties.

After a fascinating day on the job of familiarization and meeting my new associates, a casual check of the weather with Los Angeles Flight Service revealed bad news. I was in for a repeat performance. A heavy blanket of fog was already rolling in over Oceanside and all of the coastal cities. For a more accurate check on the weather I called my wife. She confirmed that fog was indeed present. She couldn't see the waves only a hundred feet away. We both agreed that she would become independently wealthy if a return trip were attempted that evening.

That night the inexpensive (but not cheap, you understand) motel room was also quite an experience. The proprietor's look bordered on fishy when I checked in without any luggage. Somehow, he didn't look like he'd go for any type of "Gee, I got fogged in" story. After all, the evening weather was gorgeous in Van Nuys. His eyes sparkled with insincerity as he said, "That'll be eighteen dollars, please—in advance."

He put me in the room right next to the office. The fact that I'd walked in without a car probably didn't help matters much, either. Since the rooms were built before the telephone was invented, I had to borrow an alarm clock. The $10 deposit seemed a bit steep; it became patently obvious that he didn't trust me.

It was a long night. It was difficult not to listen to the intimate domestic situation in the next room, and every time I'd drift off to sleep some guy four rooms down would clear his throat. "If commuting by air is going to be like this," I thought, "there's going to be one Cessna up for sale very shortly."

Next morning, after a fighter pilot's breakfast of two aspirins, a cup of coffee, and a Twinkie, I hailed a taxi. Even the cab driver gave me a fishy stare. Maybe it was the needed shave or perhaps the wrinkled shirt, which looked like it had been worn for two days, which it had. He didn't look like a man who would buy the "fogged-in" tale either. But I showed him, by only tipping thirty cents. Of course I wasn't late for work for the second day in a row, but then few people are when they spend the night a few blocks from their office.

The entire first week was a pretty grim and discouraging period. It was foggy or smoggy, or both, most of the time. I logged more actual instrument time in five days than in a whole year in the military. I did get home finally at the end of the first week, but I began to feel like the coach whose varsity players had all been caught cheating. It really wasn't his fault but it still made for a losing season.

The next week the sun came out and the name of the game changed. Warm desert winds blew in and you could see fifty miles in every direction. The Channel Islands looked to be within spitting distance. My whole attitude took on a new light. Now I was telling jokes and laughing. Good flying weather can do that, particularly when you're on a twice-a-day schedule. In the next six months I was late only once, and then just by nine minutes.

I learned a lot, too, mainly about those giant airliners that went hurtling by above. We formed a pact; I didn't go above two thousand feet in their back yard, and they didn't come below. This worked quite well. Actually, my flight path went under the approach routes to the Los Angeles Airport and far enough out to ensure a safe separation.

The traffic-watch helicopters and fixed-wing aircraft were another story. There were at least six or seven airborne observers, each reporting the latest traffic conditions below to their respective radio and TV stations. To avoid the unpleasantness of midair collisions, each pilot would relay his (or her) position about every five minutes. After a while, we knew where all the other guys were. Since I was one of very few daily commuters, Cessna 79 Sierra became rather well known, inasmuch as we all monitored the same radio frequency.

Innocently, one morning I'd reported a bad accident on the 405 San Diego Freeway. Bruce Wayne, who reported traffic for KFI, the radio station, credited the accident report to "Don Tooker in 79 Sierra." Celebrity status had arrived. Most of the other radio and television reporters would use my inputs, even when reporting that all freeways in my neck of the woods were clear. Many employees at Lockheed would tune in to their respective stations on their way to work. But one thing was certain, calling in traffic congestion sure broke up the monotony of the morning and evening commutes.

Solving the small-plane menace was not so easy. There were, and are, literally hundreds of gnatlike light aircraft that swarm around Southern California when the weather is good. It's like that hula-hoop fad some years back. Now all those kids have grown up and own a lightplane. The best solution was to maintain a swivel-mounted head and to avoid flying at exactly a thousand feet. For some reason, that's a very popular altitude. It's like the fast lane on the freeway—everyone prefers it.

A lot of people, mostly my lovely wife, asked how much it

D. K Tooker, dressed for work at Lockheed and ready to fly from Oceanside to Van Nuys—two hours a day for three years.

costs to fly to work. Is it cheaper than driving? The answer is, "Bring your checkbook." It became obvious rather early in the commuting game that it does indeed cost more than driving, but the convenience and desirability of being home every night was worth the additional expense. The more than two hundred thousand lightplane owners in the Los Angeles area would agree with me that flying is both a great sport and a pretty expensive one. As a hobby, it's still cheaper than drinking, but more expensive than water skiing. I'd place it somewhere between girls and yachting. Even so, the cost was not prohibitive, given the circumstances.

Flying costs are expressed in dollars per flying hour. For example, in 1968 the Cessna 150 cost about $15 per hour to operate. This amount included gas and oil, tie-down or hangar costs, maintenance, insurance, and engine overhaul. You have to set aside so much per flight hour or come up way short when the engine time runs out. Unlike a car, periodic inspections and overhauls are an FAA regulation. Thus it cost me about $30 a day to fly to work. So, not counting depreciation, which may be like ignoring a snowstorm at a baseball game, it wasn't prohibitive cost-wise. That's hard to explain to a thrifty wife. In fact, it's hard to explain to the other kind. To summarize, it costs about three times more to fly than drive to work.

Luckily, some relief surfaced. It wasn't aspirin or a second mortgage or the Peace Corps. I simply leased back the teeny-weeny commuter to the FBO (fixed base operator) at the Oceanside Airport. It turned out that they needed extra planes to rent for flight instruction on the weekends. Since I needed 79 Sierra during the week, it was marriage made in the skies. In this way I was able to recoup some income, which helped ease the financial burden. The FBO even threw in a free tie-down and, of course, I never bothered them to "borrow" the airplane on weekends. No busman's holiday there.

It took some getting used to—the foggy mornings, the hurtling jets, and the driving rains at night. Although my handshakes were still occasionally clammy, it was a small price to pay for being able to come home every night. The twelve-hour days weren't so bad either; it was still better than my son's paper route.

A good thing happened about six months into my airborne commuting program. A paying passenger, Harry Alter, showed up. He was an engineer who worked for the same aerospace company and had been driving up from San Diego on Sunday evenings and home after the week's work on Friday nights. He liked his beachside home, too. He'd heard about my airways exploits on the radio and had asked me at work one day if there might be an extra seat available. There was. He'd meet me every morning at 6:00 A.M. at the Oceanside Airport, park his car next to mine, and ride in the right seat on our way to work. He shared the gasoline costs quite fairly, and now breaking even financially was almost a reality.

Harry was retiring in two years. He appreciated being able to be home every night except, of course, when the Oceanside Airport was fogged in. The field had no instrument landing approach because it was situated in a small valley with hills on both sides, as I had discovered during that first zero-zero takeoff a half year earlier. Harry couldn't fly and didn't want to, even while I shaved on the way to work. I guess he figured some kind of magic was involved and wanted no part of it. Apparently, he had complete faith in my airplane driving skills. So did I.

One of the most frequently asked questions from my coworkers was, "What do you do in bad weather?" I usually replied, with a superior air, "The mails will go through." And, in fact, in three years of commuting, bad weather forced me into ground transportation only once. We were one hour late then—but so were most of the commercial flights into the greater Los Angeles complex that day. It was one heck of a storm. One day in three years, one might say, "ain't bad."

But there was one time when it was really nasty out—not bad enough to keep the Tooker Commuter grounded, but bad enough to get our attention. It was late February and of course, quite dark by 5:30 P.M. when we got airborne at Van Nuys Airport. We'd filed the mandatory hard IFR flight plan and the aerology report wasn't too bad—cloud tops at fifteen thousand feet with some icing reported. Nothing Harry and I couldn't handle. Of course, the little Cessna could not reach an altitude above the clouds even if it wanted to, and it didn't. Besides, we carried no oxygen equipment. As for the icing conditions, we had carburetor heat just in case.

After reaching our assigned altitude of five thousand feet, we began taking the many vectors directed by Los Angeles Center. These course changes were needed to get us safely through the ever crowded skies.

"Cessna Seven Nine Sierra, request you climb to and maintain seven thousand feet. Report reaching seven thousand feet."

"Roger, Center," I responded. The air became a little more turbulent as we gained altitude but, more importantly, it got colder. We reached our newly assigned altitude and so reported.

"Cessna Seven Nine Sierra, we have airliner traffic at your nine o'clock, can you climb to and maintain nine thousand feet?"

"That's affirm, Center, but that's about our maximum."

"OK, Seven Nine Sierra, report reaching nine thousand. Your position is now twenty-six miles north northeast of the El Toro VOR"—Variable Omni Range, a navigational aid.

At nine thousand feet I reported as directed. Harry seemed quite relaxed, but I wasn't, as an increased amount of carburetor heat was necessary. This was needed to prevent ice from building up in the venturi portion of the carburetor, thus preventing the engine from receiving sufficient air to perform. The tension on the left side of the cockpit increased proportionately with the turbulence from the moisture-laden clouds. Harry looked like he might go to sleep at any moment.

"Cessna Seven Nine Sierra. You are now fifteen miles northeast of El Toro VOR. Are you maintaining nine thousand feet, over?" I glanced at the altimeter only to see that we had slipped down to 8,700 feet.

"Ah, Roger, Center. I'm a tad below assigned altitude, but I'm at full throttle. We may have picked up some ice."

"Understand, Seven Nine Sierra. Are you requesting a lower altitude?" Before I could answer, the engine quit cold. Literally. We'd run out of available carburetor heat, not to mention power.

"Mayday, Mayday, Los Angeles Center. Seven Nine Sierra. We've lost all power. Cannot maintain altitude."

"Roger, Seven Nine Sierra. We're clearing all airspace below you. Suggest vector two one zero degrees immediately to clear mountains to your left." (This was the Saddleback Mountain Range.) The silence in the cockpit was very noticeable, and I could see that the recent turn of events had finally captured Harry's attention. Still, he said nothing.

"Cessna Seven Nine Sierra, this is Los Angeles Center. Suggest you switch to 124.5 now and contact El Toro Approach Control. They are aware of your emergency."

"Thanks, Center, for your help. Switching now." The radio knobs were spun to the new frequency.

"El Toro Approach, this is Seven Nine Sierra, passing through seven thousand feet, heading two one zero with complete engine failure. Pretty sure it's iced up."

"Roger, Seven Nine Sierra, we have you in radar contact. To verify, squawk emergency on your transponder. Say what type of aircraft, please."

"Seven Nine Sierra is a very quiet Cessna One-Fifty. Are we clear of the Saddleback Range, over?"

"That's affirm, Seven Nine Sierra. You're headed toward the coast between Laguna Beach and Dana Point. What are your intentions, over?" At least I had a picture of where we were in relation to the ground; a moment's pause while I thought things over. We were going down, but the big question, remembering it was night time, was . . . where?

"Ah, El Toro Approach, I'd like to be vectored to a position parallel to the coast just off shore if that's possible. We'll ditch just off the beach but close enough to swim in." The radio was silent for a moment, while Approach Control and I thought about what had just been said.

"Roger, Seven Nine Sierra, understand you intend to ditch. We can give you radar vectors that should put you over the water but no guarantee how far off the beach." The controller then added, "We've launched the air-sea rescue chopper." This was the first good news in a while. Looking at Harry, "Can you swim?" I asked, trying to sound casual to my trusting, paying passenger.

"Pretty much," he responded, leaving me to wonder what "pretty much" meant. We were now passing three thousand feet, leaving us with less than four minutes to get ready for the cold water waiting below. I needed to brief him.

"Harry, we'll be setting down on the ocean in a couple of minutes. Don't know if we can see the reefs and cliffs along the beach. Too risky to try a landing on the sand. At least the water's flat." He nodded, as if this was just another routine procedure like a landing at Van Nuys.

"When we ditch, the wheels"—which were nonretractable—"will probably cause us to flip over on our back. Not to worry. We'll get out on your side"—there being only the one door. "As soon as we're stopped and settled, pull that emergency door-release lever and push the door out of the way. Then undo your seat belt and exit the aircraft. The aircraft should float for a few seconds. Bring your seat cushion along. It'll provide some buoyancy. Remember, I'll be right behind you, and we'll swim ashore through the surf. We'll be OK," I added, trying to sound reassuring. He finally said something that sounded like "Well, okay," but a new voice on the radio cut him off.

"Seven Nine Sierra, this is Rescue Chopper Zero One, airborne approaching Dana Point. What's your altitude, over?"

"Passing twelve hundred feet. I think I see some lights below through the clouds. Dark ocean on the right."

"Roger Seven Nine Sierra. We should be a little behind you. You still intend to ditch?"

"Affirm, Zero One. Not much choice." I hoped my voice didn't sound panicky. I gave Harry a thumbs up, but he only stared at my thumb like it was a beacon. At least *he* wasn't panicky.

As we broke through the cloud layer, I was surprised to find reasonably good visibility, five to six miles, and the shoreline was on the left where it was supposed to be. As I pushed the mike button down to talk to Zero One, a new sound entered our quiet cockpit. The engine had suddenly come back to life as if to say, "O ye of little faith."

"This is Seven Nine Sierra. I've got some power. Guess the ice has melted at the lower altitude."

"Bravo! Way to go!"—an informal congratulatory transmission from the rescue chopper. The El Toro controller's radio had been blocked out by the terrain as we'd descended below the required line-of-sight communications altitude.

Harry's expression had really never changed, as far as I could tell in the dim cockpit lighting. But mine sure did. It was all smiles, as I asked Zero One to advise Approach Control that we'd regained power at about three hundred feet and were continuing on to our Oceanside destination, and they could cancel our instrument flight plan because we were proceeding VFR (by visual flight rules).

"That's a big Roger, Seven Nine Sierra. Would you like an escort for a few miles?"

"Negative, Zero One. I think this airliner will get us there now. Thanks again for your kind attention. Glad we didn't need your services." He clicked his mike in response and flew along with us a short distance anyway, until we could both see the lights of Oceanside reflecting on the clouds above the city.

Harry and I landed about ten minutes later without further incident. After we had tied down the aircraft and had headed to our respective cars, he said: "Same time tomorrow, Don?" sounding as if he'd been prepared for a night ditching in a very cold ocean all of this life.

"Sure, Harry, same time, same station. Have a safe drive home." I didn't know what else to say.

After parking the car in front of our house on the beach, I took a deep breath of relief and savored that "glad to be home" feeling. In the living room, my wife greeted me with her usual, "Good flight, honey?"

You guessed it; I told her, "Pretty much so."

EPILOGUE

The air commute continued until the end of the third year, without incident. Late in 1970, Lockheed lost the Cheyenne attack helicopter contract and laid off 2,800 workers—including, unfortunately, Harry and me. He retired, I sold the Cessna, and my wife was very, very pleased. I commuted to my next job by car, like all the rest. It was back to monotony again.

ABOUT THE AUTHOR

D. K. Tooker, who served in three wars, began his military career in 1943 as a naval aviation cadet and retired as a United States Marine Corps lieutenant colonel in 1968. During his twenty-five years on active duty, he flew more than seven thousand hours in thirty-six types of fixed-wing aircraft and nineteen models of helicopter. He has operated from three straight-deck and three angled-deck carriers and has logged 133 combat missions. His decorations include two Distinguished Flying Crosses, ten Air Medals, two Navy Commendation Medals, and the Presidential Unit Citation.

He has written articles about his flying experiences for several popular and professional magazines, including *Reader's Digest*. His book *The Second-Luckiest Pilot*, published in 2000, is now in its third printing. It has been endorsed by Chuck Yeager, Clive Cussler, and Joe Foss, the leading Marine Corps ace in World War II.

He and his wife live in Orange, California.